A growing number of people are seeking the depth-dimension of Christianity. In *A Season of Silence*, Joshua Rey offers a gentle introduction to silent prayer, which will be a great help to many. With great humility, the author speaks of his own journey within a life-changing way of prayer, providing down-to-earth encouragement while making it clear that the wisdom and healing processes of silence are available for all of us.

Chris Whittington, Founder and lead teacher,
School of Contemplative Life

Joshua Rey's beautiful book is a gift to anyone who wishes seriously to deepen a life of faith. Its step-by-step approach offers a simple and inviting way in to the practice of silent prayer. It is wonderfully readable, frequently entertaining and wears its considerable learning very lightly. Proudly mundane and rooted in common sense, it leads the reader towards truths both practical and profound.

Peter Groves, Vicar, St Mary Magdalen Oxford

In our noisy world, deliberately cultivating and seeking out silence is more important than ever. As Christians we know this, but we're so very rarely guided through the mechanics of how to enter into it with the kind of companionable advice Joshua Rey provides here. Using poetry, Scripture, ancient wisdom and contemporary creative images, *A Season of Silence* gradually eases the reader into the silence, increasing our tolerance to a practice that is as deceptively difficult as it is nourishing.

Jayne Manfredi, Author and Broadcaster

Joshua Rey shows us the Christian truth that if we pay attention, attention pays us back. There is an attention of the heart, rather than of the mind and, for this to be generative we need a deep and disturbing silence. It sounds formidable – but this author is on your side and guides the way with a refreshing humanity.

Mark Oakley, Dean, Southwark Cathedral

A Season of Silence

A Season of Silence

Deep Listening in a Noisy World

Joshua Rey

CANTERBURY
PRESS

© Joshua Rey 2025

Published in 2025 by the Canterbury Press Norwich

Editorial office
3rd Floor, Invicta House,
110 Golden Lane,
London EC1Y 0TG, UK
www.canterburypress.co.uk

Canterbury Press is an imprint of Hymns Ancient & Modern Ltd
(a registered charity)

Hymns Ancient & Modern® is a registered trademark of
Hymns Ancient & Modern Ltd
13A Hellesdon Park Road, Norwich,
Norfolk NR6 5DR, UK

All rights reserved. No part of this publication may be reproduced,
stored in a retrieval system, or transmitted,
in any form or by any means, electronic, mechanical,
photocopying or otherwise, without the prior permission of
the publisher, Canterbury Press.

The author has asserted his right under the Copyright, Designs and
Patents Act 1988 to be identified as the Author of this Work

British Library Cataloguing in Publication data

A catalogue record for this book is available
from the British Library

Scripture quotations (other than the psalms) are from New Revised
Standard Version Bible: Anglicized Edition, copyright © 1989, 1995
National Council of the Churches of Christ in the United States of America.
Used by permission. All rights reserved worldwide.
Psalms are taken from Common Worship: Daily Prayer, London: Church
House Publishing, © The Archbishops' Council. Used by permission.

ISBN: 978-1-78622-661-7

EU GPSR Authorised Representative
LOGOS EUROPE, 9 rue Nicolas Poussin, 17000, LA ROCHELLE, France
E-mail: Contact@logoseurope.eu

No part of this book may be used or reproduced in any manner for the
purpose of training artificial intelligence technologies or systems.

Typeset by Regent Typesetting

Contents

Introduction: 40 Daily Reflections on Silent Prayer		1
Day 1	A Free Holiday	5
Day 2	The Mystery of Silence	8
Day 3	Fear of the Dark	12
Day 4	Listen	15
Day 5	Strength Made Perfect	18
Day 6	A World of Noise	21
Day 7	A Silent Rebellion	24
Day 8	The Listening Body	27
Day 9	Sitting Down	30
Day 10	Sitting Up	33
Day 11	Breathe	36
Day 12	Breathing	39
Day 13	Looking at What?	42
Day 14	When?	45
Day 15	Where?	48
Day 16	Dostoevsky's Polar Bear	51
Day 17	Be Here Now	54
Day 18	The End of the Beginning	57

Day 19	A Body Scan	60
Day 20	Something to Do	63
Day 21	Something to Say	66
Day 22	Pole Vaulting in Zero G	69
Day 23	Groundhog Mountaineering	72
Day 24	Puppies, Ripples and Toddlers	75
Day 25	Other People	79
Day 26	Listening in the Psalms	82
Day 27	Listening Beyond	85
Day 28	Portable Peace	88
Day 29	Just Doing Nothing	91
Day 30	Smiling	94
Day 31	Looking Out	97
Day 32	Embrace Boredom	100
Day 33	Walking Away from the Looking Glass House	103
Day 34	Because the Other is Worth It	106
Day 35	Listening Outward	109
Day 36	Pre-flight Checklist	112
Day 37	Listening Towards	115
Day 38	The Listening God	118
Day 39	The Life of God	121
Day 40	No Longer I that Liveth	124

Further Reading   127

Introduction

40 Daily Reflections on Silent Prayer

Let me come clean at the start: I'm not that good at silent prayer. My first career was in investment banking, which is not a contemplative environment. Funnily enough, though, it was while I was working in the City that I became a Christian. I found that two of my closest colleagues went to a lunchtime service every Tuesday, and for the first time I thought 'What if it's true?' It started to annoy me; I wanted to figure it out. I read, argued and thought. I even prayed a bit, along the lines of 'I don't believe in you but if you do exist, would you please reveal yourself to me?'

This was the start of a long story I needn't bore you with, which led to baptism, swapping banking for aid work and, after several other steps and missteps, ending up a vicar in south London. But from the start, faith was a subject of thought, word, action, research, inquiry. These are good things but as a young Christian I was never drawn to the 'yet more' of contemplation. Even at theological college the clever kids went in for silence, but I always preferred to read my Bible or get on my knees and talk to God.

Once ordained, however, I started taking an annual retreat in a Trappist monastery. There was a lot of silence. I didn't get it, but I joined in. I also put myself under a wise spiritual director, who advised daily silent prayer. Again, I complied. My mind wandered. I thought about the Scriptures ... what I had to do that day ... and ... wasn't quite sure what was going on. Then I started working as Chaplain to the Bishop of

Southwark, a notoriously good listener. He turned me on to the power of listening: not just an interpersonal skill, but a spiritual discipline: 'it is from listening that true harmony emerges'.

Now it started making sense. Silence that was just the absence of sound was a nothing. Silence that was alert listening seemed like a something – a something worth digging into. It was hard, though. Nature abhors a vacuum. I fill silence with mental words, ideas, images, hopes, regrets, reflections, thoughts ... how interesting it is that the mind wanders ... how strangely hard it is to let go of a train of thought such as this one I am now thinking ... how interesting it would be to write a book about these problems ...

You see my issue. If you're *doing* silent prayer, actively concentrating on it all the time, it's not silent prayer. For silent prayer is not just the absence of vibrations in the air. It is a deeper, inner silence, in which the mind's monologue is allowed to cease as well. This is hard. Thus, I went on thinking and reading about it, which is so much easier. Something went in, though. Sometimes, despite myself, I got past the thinking and reading. My daily time of silence had more to it and enriched other parts of life. As is often the way with clergy when we think we're on to something I spoke of it more, commended it to others, led the occasional retreat or Lent course. At length, it became this book.

I hope you are clear now that you are not reading the reflections of an adept. I am no sage in a mountain cave, no wise abbot steeped in decades of cloistered calm. Books have been written by such spiritual athletes, who live at altitudes I only glimpse from where my lungs and limbs give out. There are some in the Further Reading section at the end of the book and I encourage you to read them.

The deficiencies of this book, however, may also be its strength. Entering into true silent prayer is not easy, but really if I can do it, you can too. However baffling and uncomfortable you may find it, I get you. Yet I'm here to tell you, this can be unfathomably life-giving if you will commit and persevere.

There's nothing fancy here. We are dealing with transcendent mysteries, but our way into them is down to earth. We are going to learn to sit, breathe and listen, here and now. And we are going to sit, breathe and listen, here and now every day. There are 40 reflections. Each day you read a reflection and then sit, breathe and listen, here, now. The first four days you do that for 2 minutes. Days 5 to 8 you do 3 minutes, then Days 9 to 12 it's 4 minutes. And so on – until for the last week or so you are up to 10 minutes a day. At the end of 40 days, over to you. Keep doing it. Just 10 minutes a day. Sit, breathe, listen: be here now. I hope by then you will have learnt a few things about how it works, why it's worth doing, and what it all means.

Forty days should be long enough for this to start becoming a habit, and that will help embed it in your day. Forty days is also a handy number if you want to do this in Lent. But you can do it any time: combining the penitential season of Advent with the first few weeks of New Year would be great – there will be a cultural momentum behind a wholesome new resolution. You can follow this book alone, or with others. You could run it as a course for your church. There are resources to help with all of this on the website that goes with the book, www.seasonofsilence.org.

If this sounds mundane, then good. Explore these mysteries with me and you explore with a frequently puzzled, backsliding, fairly practical, material person living an ordinary life with no special gifts or powers. This is not a transcendent work. There is no arcane wisdom. I just want to help you acquire a practice I know will be life-giving, in the fullest sense of 'life': a deepening of your relationship with God as he reveals himself in Christ through the Holy Spirit.

This has always been the aim, but I never found how to say what this book is, with the correct mix of fun, serious intent and practicality, until I sent it to David Shervington, Publishing Director at Canterbury Press, and he said, 'It's a kind of "Couch to 5k" for silence.' That's exactly what it is. Let's get started.

Day 1

A Free Holiday

Do you wish you had a cottage on a mountainside, a cabin by the lake, a clifftop villa? Somewhere to go whenever you wanted rest, refreshment and peace?

Well, you do. We all do. If we will only take the key and turn it in the lock.

You may be reading this at the start of Advent or Lent. You may have come to it looking for something serious, a spiritual challenge. You will not be disappointed. It will not be all ha-ha-ha, he-he-he. There will be discipline. There will be renunciation. By grace we will enter deeper into the fathomless depth of God's life, go a few steps up the infinite mountain, swim a few strokes towards the limitless horizon. We reach the deep and life-giving joy that comes from true and silent prayer through a pilgrimage that can be long and hard.

But I want to start with an introductory offer. This is going to be great! We are going somewhere you will simply like and enjoy. You are going to find a place of rest where you can renew your strength and peace of mind. It's not the only thing you will find, nor the best, but I hope it sounds fairly obviously attractive. That's the introductory offer: a free holiday, whenever and wherever you want it. If that sounds worth having, let us go forward together in the next six weeks and learn to put the key in the lock of our holiday home.

That's almost it for today. Just three more things to do, please, before we start in earnest tomorrow.

First, glance at the texts below. Each day there will be some Scripture, or a hymn, or some lines of poetry, or some wise prose. There will also be a question for reflection, and a short prayer. Please read them, and use them as you find helpful.

Second, please think about how you are going to time your silence. Most people use the timer on their smartphone. Do make sure the ring tone is a gentle one. If you have the technical skill, use a piece of music or something else that will bring you back out of silence without shattering your peace. You could use a digital oven timer, but they bleep rather alarmingly. Better not use a clock or watch because you have to glance at it which is going to break things up.

You have a few days to get this right, but by Day 5 I'd like you to have a system. Please make sure you do no less than the time specified, but not too much longer. In the long run you may do without a timer altogether, but it's best to start with one. Silence often feels longer than it is.

Third, please now be silent for 2 minutes.

Nothing more than that for now. Just say and do nothing for 2 minutes. All sorts of other things will be going on. We'll come to them as we go on. Today's task is just that: be silent for 2 minutes.

Our journey has begun.

2 minutes

From *Meditations*, Marcus Aurelius

People are always looking for somewhere to retreat to: villages, unspoilt coastline, mountainsides. You too, my soul, long for the same things. But this is idiotic, because whenever you want you can always go away inside yourself. Nowhere a person can go away to is so calm and free from worry as one's own inner self …

Question for reflection

If you were offered the superpower that you could travel to any spot on Earth instantly, any time you chose, and remain there for up to half an hour at a time, but you had to pick just one destination – where would you opt to have as your place of retreat?

Prayer

God of peace:
thank you that you have good purposes for me;
thank you for the gift of peace and stillness;
open my heart and mind to receive it
as I make my journey with you.

Day 2

The Mystery of Silence

Have you ever swum over the edge of an underwater cliff? For the full drama, swim with snorkel and face mask looking down as you swim out. At first, the seabed falls away gently. You could still dive for a shell and bring it to the surface. You see rocks and seaweed and fish flitting about or coiling in shoals beneath you. Sunbeams catch swirling particles of sand. A busy scene, light and colour.

Ahead you see a lip in the seabed and a deeper blue beyond. Before you know it, the rocks drop away beneath you and you swim out over the full depth of the coastal seabed. You can see nothing now but the flicker of a remote fish or a pale sunbeam tapering off into darkness. Below all is blue-black, seemingly empty and silent. You could swim much deeper here if you could hold your breath long enough. But there is no swimming to the bottom now.

It is a moment of wonder and sometimes one of alarm or fear.

We may encounter this awe, wonderful and terrible, as we journey into silence. There is depth. Not depth we get to the bottom of, but real depth, depth unknowable. In true silence there will always be something we cannot reach, something beyond.

Or will there? I don't want to close down your experience of silence. This is a voyage of discovery. You have to find out for yourself. Start from where you are. I wonder what silence is like for you, whether you welcome it or find it daunting, whether you find it mysterious or no more than the absence of noise. All the same, please be open to the possibility that there is more to this than you think. Be alert to the moment when you swim out over the depths. Be ready for when you can go deeper than you expected.

Floating in the shallows among the flickering colours of fish and the infinite textures of seaweed crowding the rocks is lovely. Just as sitting with our thoughts, memories and hopes, letting the mind wander like a grazing pony, is a fine way to spend a sunny afternoon. Never underestimate this – we shall speak more of it as we go on. Remember, though, there is always more depth.

That is what we are going for in these 40 days. Sometimes the dive may be a lung-burster. We don't know what we will find, or what will find us. When we come up we will swim with greater ease in the shallows – and swimming in the shallows can help us dive. But we are seeking the depths. Don't anticipate, don't think what the depths are going to be like. Simply bear in mind that they are there.

Again, have a read of the text, answer the question if that helps, pray the prayer if you wish. Then, please take 2 more minutes to be silent. No agenda or expectations. Let it be what it is.

2 minutes

Psalm 46

God is our refuge and strength,
a very present help in trouble;
Therefore we will not fear, though the earth be moved,
and though the mountains tremble in the heart of the sea;
Though the waters rage and swell,
and though the mountains quake at the towering seas.
There is a river whose streams make glad the city of God,
the holy place of the dwelling of the Most High.
God is in the midst of her;
therefore shall she not be removed;
God shall help her at the break of day.
The nations are in uproar and the kingdoms are shaken,
but God utters his voice and the earth shall melt away.
The Lord of hosts is with us;
the God of Jacob is our stronghold.
Come and behold the works of the Lord,
what destruction he has wrought upon the earth.
He makes wars to cease in all the world;
he shatters the bow and snaps the spear
and burns the chariots in the fire.
'Be still, and know that I am God;
I will be exalted among the nations;
I will be exalted in the earth.'
The Lord of hosts is with us;
the God of Jacob is our stronghold.

Question for reflection

If you were told you had to spend 20 minutes in a silent room with no books or pictures or phone or computer, nothing but a comfortable armchair, would you be filled with delight or dread, or something in between?

Prayer

Eternal and loving God
open my heart to know
the heights and depths of who you are
as I come to you in silence:
I ask this through Jesus Christ.

Day 3

Fear of the Dark

Swimming over the edge of the underwater cliff may be daunting. But there is nothing in depth itself, however fathomless and awesome, to menace us. Yet for many of us silence is uncomfortable. True deep silence can be scary. It strips away all that distracts us from things we find hard.

The first thing that comes to us out of the dark may be something we have been trying to avoid. Regret. Fear. Failures and disappointed hopes. Doubts about those we love. Doubts about our own strength. Doubts about God. The reality that how things are is never quite how they could or should be. True silence is the opposite of putting our fingers in our ears. Letting go of surface noise opens us up rather than closing us down, and that makes it impossible to pretend everything is OK. If there is something anxious or sorrowful we don't want to think about, silent prayer may let it come to us.

Above all, in silence we encounter that sense some of us have of 'Is this all there is?' … 'What is the point?' … 'Is any of this real?' … 'Do I really exist?' As T. S. Eliot puts it, 'the conversation rises and slowly fades into silence … leaving only the growing terror of nothing to think about' (Eliot, *Four Quartets*, p. 17).

This is one reason why the journey into silence is a good one for Advent or Lent. Penitential seasons are times to push through resistance, traverse deserts and rocky places, persevere through harsh weather. Be of good courage: the light shines in the darkness and the darkness does not overcome it. But Lent and Advent are times to press on through the darkness.

Remember this when you meet resistance on the journey into silence. When it is hard is often the moment something good can come into being if you persevere. Sometimes God is most truly present when all that is good and hopeful appears to have vanished and we go on through it. Thus do we come out to the light. Be aware also that sometimes the hardest challenges can be the trivial ones. Facing our deepest fears may feel heroic, which gives us strength. Recalling tiny moments of shame and failure or dreading the hard conversation at work can be where we meet the real resistance.

Welcome these moments. They are signs we are opening ourselves up to something deeper. Happy and blameless people may enter into silence right away. Most of us are going to hear something we don't like when we open the ears of our hearts. The key is, when unwelcome thoughts come, when we meet something on the road we wish had stayed in the shadows, know that this is not a barrier but a signpost. We are on the right road.

Now, another 2 minutes of silence.

2 minutes

From 'Dover Beach' by Matthew Arnold

The sea is calm tonight.
The tide is full, the moon lies fair
Upon the straits; on the French coast the light
Gleams and is gone; the cliffs of England stand,
Glimmering and vast, out in the tranquil bay.
Come to the window, sweet is the night-air!
Only, from the long line of spray
Where the sea meets the moon-blanched land,
Listen! you hear the grating roar
Of pebbles which the waves draw back, and fling,
At their return, up the high strand,
Begin, and cease, and then again begin,
With tremulous cadence slow, and bring
The eternal note of sadness in.

Question for reflection

Are there thoughts or feelings you try to blot out with noise of one kind or another?

Prayer (from *Common Worship Daily Prayer*)

O God my protector,
I give into your hands my unfinished tasks,
my unsolved problems,
and my unfulfilled hopes;
for you alone are my sure defence
and bring me lasting peace
in Jesus Christ our Lord.

Day 4

Listen

So far, you have simply been silent for 2 minutes. We have reflected on what silence may offer and what may be hard about it. In a few days we will think about why true silence, which has always been a life-giving discipline, is an urgent necessity today. Then we will spend a week or so on practical things like breathing and sitting, where and when. Then we will tackle the paradox of silent prayer: hard to do because if we are *doing* something we are not being truly silent. After that we will talk about how you can expand this beyond a daily personal discipline – which will in turn enrich the discipline.

By then you will be a week from the end of the book, your daily time of silence will be 10 minutes, and all of this much more familiar. Only at that point will we go deeper into what is really happening, to the heart of the 'true silence' I have spoken of in the last few days.

Today, however, I want to tip my hand. I want to tell you the 'secret'. But there is no secret. Like so many elements in the life well lived it's not that complicated. It's just, sometimes, quite hard. I'm sorry if you wanted to keep the big reveal for the end. No time for a spoiler alert, for the clue is in today's title.

Listen.
Listen.
Listen.

In the beginning of Creation, God spoke: the unformed universe listened, and took form.

Samuel's life of prophecy began when Eli taught him to say 'Speak, Lord, for your servant is listening' (1 Sam. 3.9).

When the people of Israel fall away from God, the prophets call them to listen again.

The Psalmist meditates 'On God alone my soul in stillness waits' (Ps. 62.1).

On the mount of Transfiguration the voice from the cloud declares 'This is my Son, the Beloved, listen to him!' (Mark 9.7).

Jesus says again and again to the crowds, 'Let anyone with ears to hear listen!' (Mark 4.9).

The Rule of St Benedict, that great store of Christian wisdom, begins 'Hearken continually within thine heart' (St Benedict, *Rule*, p. 1).

Listening is the heart of it. Listening is the solution to the paradox that all we can do is do, but true silence is not doing. Listening makes the private discipline of silent prayer useful in the day-to-day world. Listening links silence to the one in whose presence we are silent. Listening is what makes silence the true silence we seek.

As I said in the Introduction, it was the notion of listening that first turned me on to silent prayer. The simple absence of sound felt like nothing much. There are many such silences. The silence after a car crash. The silence of sneaking up on someone. The silence of thinking what to say next. The silence of boredom (though we shall redeem boredom on Day 32). These things are not the silence we seek.

When you realize that in silent prayer we are listening, it make more sense. Listening is true silence. In listening we renounce not only exterior sound, but the inner noise of thinking, planning, analysing, remembering and expecting. But it is not a void. Listening silence is fuller and richer than blank silence; fuller and richer than any amount of sound.

Now 2 more minutes of silence – and please decide that for these 2 minutes you will *listen.*

2 minutes

From Psalm 78

Hear my teaching, O my people;
incline your ears to the words of my mouth.
I will open my mouth in a parable;
I will pour forth mysteries from of old,
Such as we have heard and known,
which our forebears have told us.
We will not hide from their children,
but will recount to generations to come,
the praises of the Lord and his power
and the wonderful works he has done.

Question for reflection

When listening to someone, how hard or easy do you find it to listen without thinking what you will say next?

Prayer

Open the ears of my heart, O God:
give me patience and courage
not to fill the silence with my own words
but to attend
to all that you ask of me
to all that you will to give.

Day 5

Strength Made Perfect

What can you do without the power of hearing? You can throw and catch a ball, pick someone's pocket, read a map and see the whole journey laid out before you, punch someone on the nose, cut down a tree, drive a car.

None of these is possible if you can hear, but lose the power of sight. Instead, you can sing in tune with everyone else, join freely in conversation, sense a hidden sorrow, inhabit the life of a forest at night, tell when the baby's awake.

Sight is the sense by which we control the world around us. By seeing we grasp. Seeing helps us succeed. We use seeing to make and carry out plans. It's our most technological sense.

Hearing, if we make our hearing that higher thing – listening – is no less purposeful than seeing. But it is less about *our* purposes. It is not about achieving an objective but about openness to what is going on. Listening is not passive, but it is not active in the way seeing is active. We cannot point our listening one way or another. There is less control, more risk and openness, in hearing rather than in seeing.

This openness is just what we hope for in silent prayer: openness that takes us beyond ourselves to a reality about more than our own purposes. This is how silence becomes more than the absence of sound. This is how silence becomes the true silence of silent prayer.

Of course, we can use listening to have an impact on our environment. In a few weeks we will learn to do this for the good of those around us. And seeing can be like listening. We can look with a receptive attitude – you might call this 'gazing'. In looking, we have a purpose; in gazing, we let go of the outcome. Learning to gaze, to see in a way that is like listening, can be life-giving. But gazing is not our topic – given the title of the book, you might want your money back if it were! It's simply helpful to notice other ways of being and sensing that are like listening. That may help us get the hang of listening well.

It may also help us grasp the fact that true listening silence is but an echo of a deeper reality.

Go back to the comparison between what you can do when you listen and what we can do when we see. You might not call listening powerful, yet there is deep power in it. There is something true here that goes well beyond listening prayer, but into which listening prayer can help us find a way. That's for another day, however, and this time I don't want to tip my hand – though the verses from Isaiah that follow come with a spoiler alert.

Today, let's increase our time of silence to 3 minutes and let it be a listening silence, gentle, open and receptive.

3 minutes

Isaiah 53.4–7

Surely he has borne our infirmities
   and carried our diseases;
yet we accounted him stricken,
   struck down by God, and afflicted.
But he was wounded for our transgressions,
   crushed for our iniquities;
upon him was the punishment that made us whole,
   and by his bruises we are healed.
All we like sheep have gone astray;
   we have all turned to our own way,
and the LORD has laid on him
   the iniquity of us all.

He was oppressed, and he was afflicted,
   yet he did not open his mouth;
like a lamb that is led to the slaughter,
   and like a sheep that before its shearers is silent,
so he did not open his mouth.

Question for reflection

What would you (or do you) miss most if you were to lose (or have lost) the power of hearing?

Prayer

Lord Jesus, God with us,
who cast aside worldly might
and in divine surrender
went to the cross:
I give up to you my poor strength
and ask you to make it perfect in weakness.

Day 6

A World of Noise

Saints down the ages have bathed in silent, listening prayer. They all found that it was good and brought them closer to God. But you can be sure they too found it hard.

Today, though, it is harder.

For the whole of human history except our present bit, the only sounds were voices, bells, flutes, animal cries, weather and so on. The loudest thing anyone had heard was a thunderclap. If you wanted music, you went to church or hired a band or sang. No voice had ever been heard more than a few hundred yards from the owner of the voice. No sound had ever been heard other than when it was first made.

Not so today. When did you last pass a day out of earshot of a car or a motor scooter or a plane, or go a day without streamed music, podcasts, radio news, announcements on buses, warnings at pedestrian crossings … ? Then there's the mental noise. Advertising. Headlines. X. TikTok. Even the clothes we wear are sometimes covered in writing.

This ambient noise is creepier than you think. Go into a corner shop. What do you see? Cigarettes, vodka, alcopops, scratch cards, chocolate, vapes, crisps, fizzy drinks, biscuits, convenience food. Not things any of us *need*. Not even things we like if we attend to what consuming is really like. Just things we *want*. Businesses could make money selling things we need or like. But, you know, a couple of pints of water and I'm done; I enjoy a symphony concert, but after two hours I'm ready to go home. The big money, as drug dealers have always known, is in selling us what we want irrespective of whether we need it or like it. For you will always buy more of the thing you want.

What that means is selling us stuff to stimulate the dopamine system. Dopamine, to shorten a longer story, is a brain chemical that rewards us for attending to the new, sudden or unusual. It had survival value for our ape ancestors, prompting them to keep an eye cocked for something they could eat or something that might eat them. But now we are human beings and we don't need this constant twitching of our attention. The really rewarding occupations call for intense concentration over long periods – 'deep work' (Newport, *Deep Work*).

Ironically, though, we have invented a million ways to stimulate the dopamine system that our ape ancestors never knew. Heroin, cocaine, crystal meth, tobacco, vodka, junk food, fruit machines, television. And, worst of all, the smartphone. Drug dealers sell illegal chemicals that stimulate the dopamine system. Smart drug dealers sell metal and glass boxes that do the same thing. The smartphone is a dopamine inhaler.

Learning the skill of silent, listening prayer may be our best chance of not getting sucked into this vortex. And you know what? We don't have to go on the internet or into a shop to get it. It's free. Help yourself. Take another 3 minutes now. Be at peace.

3 minutes

From *The Screwtape Letters* by C. S. Lewis

(Note: these are the words of a demon, so the exact opposite of what Lewis thinks!)

Music and silence – how I detest them both! How thankful we should be that ever since our Father entered Hell ... no square inch of infernal space and no moment of infernal time has been surrendered to either of these abominable forces, but all has been occupied by Noise – Noise, the grand dynamism, the audible expression of all that is exultant, ruthless, and virile – Noise which alone defends us from silly qualms, despairing scruples, and impossible desires. We will make the whole universe a noise in the end. We have already made great strides in this direction as regards the Earth. The melodies and silences of Heaven will be shouted down in the end. (Lewis, *Screwtape Letters*, pp. 113–14)

Question for reflection

What distracts you?

Prayer

O Holy Spirit,
still small voice of calm,
sound of sheer silence,
may I seek you in this world of noise,
and in seeking find.

Day 7

A Silent Rebellion

Imagine a world where everyone started the day with 10 minutes of intentional, listening, silent prayer.

We would become more honest, for in silence it is hard to deceive ourselves.

We would become calmer and less greedy, for in silence we start to perceive what really matters.

We would become more loving and compassionate, for in silence we face the reality that though we are of infinite value our lives matter no more than anybody else's.

Year by year, the world would change for the better.

But the only place it can start is with you.

This will be a rebellion, be sure of that. We are not, thank God, in the position of Dietrich Bonhoeffer, who stood up to the Nazis and was murdered in a concentration camp, or the unidentified 'tank man' who held up a column of T59 tanks in Tiananmen Square. Our rebellion will not cost us nearly so dear. Yet there is that against which we do need to stand up.

The market system has brought material prosperity unparalleled in the history of the world, but it sure does have its shadow side. There is a dynamic within it that creates more and more pointless desires for more and more pointless *stuff*. Our good fortune is that we don't have to buy it. In the Soviet Union, if you tried to live differently from how the system expected, the system punished you and there was nothing you could do about it. By contrast, you and I are not going to be sent to the Gulag if we don't gawp at YouTube or buy revitalizing power creme moisturizers at £79.50 for 50ml.

But by golly they are good at tricking us into doing it anyway! They spend billions on advertising. And note that they never advertise tomatoes or the novels of Jane Austen. If it has to be advertised, that is a clue that nobody would buy it on its own merits. Then there's the whole arsenal of Pester Power and Fear Of Missing Out, influencers, streaming TV, harvesting our preferences to find out what makes us want these things.

We need to stop buying stuff. So we are not complicit in sweated labour, so we stop burning down the planet, so we don't waste our own time and attention. But not buying it takes commitment and discipline. Silent listening prayer is a great way to push back – for two reasons.

First, it helps us live the truth that what we produce and consume is not who we are. There is something deeper that is there whether or not we earn or spend. Striving and planning and buying and grabbing doesn't take us where we need to be. If we are still and know that God is God, we have all we need. It's free. We just have to listen well enough to know it is there.

Second, nobody can monetize it. You don't need equipment to enter into peaceful silence. There is no merchandise. There is no fee. Life-giving attentive listening to the infinite is simply there, for all of us, if we will only let go of everything else.

3 minutes

John 2.13b–17

Jesus went up to Jerusalem. In the temple he found people selling cattle, sheep, and doves, and the money-changers seated at their tables. Making a whip of cords, he drove all of them out of the temple, both the sheep and the cattle. He also poured out the coins of the money-changers and overturned their tables. He told those who were selling the doves, 'Take these things out of here! Stop making my Father's house a market-place!' His disciples remembered that it was written, 'Zeal for your house will consume me.'

Question for reflection

Think of what you did last week – was there anything you didn't intend to do, but that you were tricked or lured into doing by a business or other organization?

Prayer

Holy Spirit,
still small voice of calm,
wind of change,
give me courage
to be a cleansing silence
in this world of noise.

Day 8

The Listening Body

You now have just over a week of simple listening silence under your belt. I hope you are getting a feel for it and have some more reasons to think it worth getting into.

Perhaps you are ready for some ideas about how to do it.

Does that sound strange? Good. For silence is about *not* doing. Does one need a special technique for this? Surely deploying a technique takes us away from silence? There is a lot in this and we shall have to come back to it again and again. For now, let me say two things.

First, as we have discussed, in true listening silence there is something more than nothing going on. It is the absence of many things, but it's making space for something real, immense and powerful. This is why I will often talk about silence and listening together. The kind of silence we are aiming for is an alert, ready, open silence – though none the less silent.

The second thing is more prosaic. Even if silence were just about nothing happening, nothing is quite hard to do. If you got a bump on the head and were out cold, you would be doing nothing, but that's not what we are aiming for. We want to be alive and awake, but not *doing*. We want to let go not just of working, spending, walking and talking, but of thinking, planning, remembering, hoping and fearing. And then we want to be here, now, present, with whatever there is.

We are going to have to work at this, and then work at *not working* – and then work at not working at not working! More later. But we have to start somewhere. And where we are going to start is with this simple truth: we are embodied.

This is a good thing, but it is going to challenge us. If we were disembodied spirits temporarily inhabiting an otherwise inert body, it might be easier to be still, by temporarily exiting the body, like a driver getting out of a car. But that is not who we are. Everything from my scalp to the soles of my feet is me. Not something I use, but who I am.

When we are present, we are physically present. When we are silent, we are bodily silent. And the one thing this means is we are never entirely silent. We are never doing nothing. All the time you are deep in listening silence, you will still be digesting, pumping blood round your veins, regulating your temperature.

This is a wonderful reality. We know God loves us and wants us to be with him in eternity. That goes for the whole of us, not just some abstract immaterial essence. Look at your hand for a moment and know that it is fearfully and wonderfully made in the image of God, the hand you will have in heaven.

As you sit in silence, please notice your body. Not in a spirit of evaluation, neither admiring nor regretful. But just being aware of what is there.

3 minutes

From Irenaeus of Lyons, *Against Heresies*, Book V, Chapter 6

That flesh which has been moulded is not a perfect human in itself, but the body of a human, and part of a human. Neither is the soul itself, considered apart by itself, the human; but it is the soul of a human, and part of a human. Neither is the spirit a human, for it is called the spirit, and not a human; but the commingling and union of all these constitutes the perfect human.

Question for reflection

Do you sense that your body is part of the whole of who you are, or do you make a distinction between 'me' and 'my body'?

Prayer

Creator God:
thank you for making me in your image;
thank you that you love all that I am.
By the power of your Holy Spirit
may all that I am
come to know all that you are.

Day 9

Sitting Down

In our times of silent listening prayer, we will be in one posture or another. Most people sit. That's what I have casually suggested, and I would guess you have been sitting for your 2 or 3 minutes up to now. That's also what I recommend long term. But depending on what you are able to do, there may be other options to consider. I would certainly say don't lie down. But some people stand, and some kneel. You could try some different postures, depending on what works for you. For now, however, let's stick with sitting.

So we are going to sit. How, then, shall we sit?

Unless you suffer from lower back pain you may not have given much thought to sitting. When you sit, you just ... sit. But this is a key part of our toolkit for silent prayer, so we are going to be intentional about it.

The key is: alert, not tense; calm, not lounging. Be comfortable, but not so comfortable you could fall asleep (which is why lying down is not so great). Choose a wooden chair (or pew) or a chair with the firmest of padding, not an armchair.

Then get it the right height. When you sit, your feet need to be flat on the floor if possible to ground you. Your thighs need to be horizontal so your weight is spread evenly and you don't put pressure on one point, which will distract you after a while.

You may have to try a few different chairs. It's worth it. I'm tall, so on a small chair I have to tuck my feet under to get my thighs flat. Then my shins are at such an angle my heels come off the ground. So I need a higher seat. If your legs are shorter than mine, your heels may not rest on the ground and the edge of the seat may dig into the backs of your knees. But there is a right chair for each of us.

Today, before your time of silent listening, please review what you are sitting on. Check that it works. If not, change it. Get a different chair or add a firm cushion or a board under the chair or under your feet depending on whether the chair is too low or too high. Then take time to shuffle and wriggle. Find the right way to put weight on your bottom and your feet. Please also keep it under review in the days to come. It's well worth your time, effort and thought to get it right. Despite what I was saying two days ago about consumerism, you might even be justified in spending some money to get the right chair. The aim is: low enough so that your feet rest flat on the ground; high enough so that your thighs are horizontal to avoid pressure points.

Today when you enter into silence be aware of sitting. For now, concentrate on bottom, hips, shins and feet: we'll talk about what's happening with the upper body tomorrow. Feel the contact between the ground and your feet. Feel the contact between the chair and your bottom and legs. Feel your weight for what it is. Gravity is always working. Notice that you do not cease to be part of the rest of the world.

We increase to 4 minutes today. Sit well.

4 minutes

Psalm 40

I waited patiently for the Lord;
he inclined to me and heard my cry.
He brought me out of the roaring pit,
out of the mire and clay;
he set my feet upon a rock and made my footing sure.

Question for reflection

Is there a difference in how it feels to sit when you have arranged your furniture, so you can plant your feet flat on the floor and your thighs flat on the chair?

Prayer

Lord Jesus
I am sitting with you
grounded on the earth that you made:
give me the grace to know you
sitting with me.

Day 10

Sitting Up

So we are sitting, grounded, weight evenly distributed, feeling gravity pointing the way to the Earth's core. Now, our aim is to sit in a way that is alert, but not tense or anxious, so we need to think about posture from the hips upwards.

If you can, please sit without leaning your back against anything. Tip your pelvis so the top is further forward than the bottom. Keep your spine straight, but now it is not quite vertical: your chin is over your thighs. Put your hands together and rest your forearms on your thighs. Let your upper arms hang loosely from your shoulders.

Again, as in sitting down, we need to jiggle about at first to get the right posture. Try leaning a long way over your knees, and feel how you are apt to slump forward. Try rocking back and feel the weight go on to the sit bones and your balance loosen. Find the middle point where you balance over mid thigh and heel.

You will need a gentle tension in the muscles of what exercise people call 'the core'. The core muscles are the ones in the middle of the body that hold everything else together: the muscles of the abdomen, lower back, bottom and upper thighs. Good core strength can help with standing up straight, picking things up, breathing well and singing. It's worth working at for health and well-being.

Many swear by the plank: weight on toes and elbows, keeping the body rigid. Some Pilates and yoga exercises do the same thing. All these need to be done with the correct level of training and supervision. My choice (which I recommend to anybody for whom it may be possible) is two barbell exercises, the squat and the deadlift. These really do have to be done correctly, for you are working with powerful forces. But if you get them right they are life-giving.

This may all sound a little unspiritual. It should not. We are embodied creatures. We have a sure and certain hope of a bodily resurrection. Spiritual and physical concerns are interwoven. One can practise silent listening prayer whatever one's physical condition. You can also practise silent prayer in a pub or while worrying about an exam (and it would probably make the pub more enjoyable and the exam easier) but you might not choose to do so if you didn't have to. Silent prayer is hard, so we try to get all the contributory factors right. Core strength is one of these. If you are able to cultivate a springiness in the core, that's one of a number of things that will help.

At any rate, let us sit if we can without leaning on anything. We are going for an attitude of mind expressed bodily. An attitude of calm readiness. If the doorbell rang, you could get up and answer it at once but you could happily go on sitting like this indefinitely. Alert, not tense. Calm, not slumped. Ready.

Please try another 4 minutes of silence today, aware of both sitting down and sitting up.

4 minutes

Luke 21.34–36

Be on guard so that your hearts are not weighed down with dissipation and drunkenness and the worries of this life, and that day does not catch you unexpectedly, like a trap. For it will come upon all who live on the face of the whole earth. Be alert at all times, praying that you may have the strength to escape all these things that will take place, and to stand before the Son of Man.

Question for reflection

How does it feel different to sit up in full awareness of the working of the muscles in your core?

Prayer

Come Holy Spirit:
make my heart, mind and body
alert and ready
to receive what you give;
to give what you ask.

Day 11

Breathe

At Creation, the Spirit of God hovered over the waters – in Hebrew this 'spirit' is *ruach*, breath or wind. At Pentecost the Holy Spirit came among the disciples with a sound like a wind. Teaching Nicodemus about the need to be born of the Spirit, Jesus speaks of wind that blows where it will. When God creates Adam, he breathes life into him.

When we breathe, we hear an echo of the Holy Spirit.

Attending to our breath is a part of making us ready for true listening prayerfulness. Many religious traditions have found this. Buddhists and Christians may differ over what (whom) they are listening to, but the Buddhist tradition of silence is one from which all can learn. Thich Nhat Hanh, a helpful guide to Buddhist practice, says 'Taking hold of your breath is itself mindfulness' (Thich Nhat Hanh, *The Miracle of Mindfulness*, p. 22).

Breathing properly and being aware of our breathing is going to be a big part of what we do. There may be (spoiler alert: there *is*) even more to it than the wonderful life-giving flow of air in and out of the lungs. But even the physical act of breathing hints at the spiritual.

Breathing is odd though. Some things we do are voluntary and intentional: play the violin, stand on one leg, drink a cup of tea. Some things we do without choice or intentional effort: digest, beat our hearts, synthesize hormones. Breathing is half one and half the other. You can hold your breath. You can pant. You can shape your mouth and tongue to turn your breath into song or speech. And you can also breathe without thinking. You can breathe while you sleep.

Tomorrow we will learn how to breathe. Today, however, let's simply pay attention to what is going on.

Notice the sensation and sound as air passes through your nose or mouth. Feel the movement of the air further down the windpipe. Breathe in. Pause and feel the pressure of air in the full lungs build. Breathe out and pause at the bottom, and feel the growing urge to breathe in again. Notice the movement of the ribs. They expand and contract a little, don't they? The sternum rides up and down like a rowing boat at anchor in a light swell.

Notice what the muscles of the chest and abdomen are doing. In theory, we know they are pushing the air in and out. But doesn't it sometimes feel a bit as though the air was coming in and out of its own accord and pushing the abdomen and chest from within? As we attend to what is going on with the muscles around the lungs, we become more and more aware of the work they are doing, and more able to be intentional about how they do it.

So now, 4 more minutes of silence please, and this time be aware of every aspect of breathing. Look all around the lungs with the mind's eye, attend to the movement of the air in and out. Pause the breath to see what that's like. Experience it.

4 minutes

Genesis 1.1–2

In the beginning when God created the heavens and the earth, the earth was a formless void and darkness covered the face of the deep, while a wind from God swept over the face of the waters.

Question for reflection

When did you last think about breathing?

Prayer

Holy Spirit,
wind that blows and we know not where,
mighty rushing wind,
breath of life:
give me grace
to know you as I breathe.

Day 12

Breathing

Today we are going to learn to breathe: to breathe as we breathed when we were babies, before we grew tense and edgy. We are going to breathe not in the top of the lungs, but deep down. This way of breathing will be central to silent prayer, and will also ripple through the other 16 hours of waking life, bringing calm and focus.

First, some anatomy. Find your lowest ribs. Feel their shape. They curve up towards the middle to meet over your belly button. You have a sheet of muscle that roughly follows that curve, dividing your torso into two compartments. Above are the lungs, below are the digestive organs. To breathe, you flex that muscle downwards, flattening it out, making more space in the lung compartment, which opens up the lungs – like drawing back the plunger of a bicycle pump.

We often don't do this to the full. We give the diaphragm a squeeze and suck air into the top of our lungs. Today we are going deeper. So try this please. Sit, as we have learnt to sit, comfortable but alert. Draw air in through your nose as though you want to smell everything. And at the same time consciously push the muscles of your abdomen out and down. Make your belly a dome. This pulls your diaphragm further down than in a casual breath. You should have a sense of forcing, firmly but not roughly, as much air as far down as possible.

Hold for a beat. Then pull the dome of your belly back in, forcing your diaphragm up and pushing the air out of the bottom of your lungs.

OK? Do that a few times.

Now next time you breathe in, push the air down, making the belly a dome as before. But when you have filled the bottom of your lungs, push your chest out and up, drawing more air into the top. Again, hold for a beat. Breathe out, starting at the bottom – rather like rolling up an airbed to get all the air out. Pull your belly in, pushing the diaphragm up, squeezing the air out of the bottom of your lungs. Draw your chest down and in. Repeat a few times.

Now, one more thing. Breathe in, fill the bottom of the lungs, lift the chest to fill the top of the lungs, then expand the ribs out to the side, filling the lungs yet fuller. Hold. Breathe out, first contracting the dome of the belly, then drawing the chest in, then collapsing the rib cage, rolling up the airbed. Repeat.

Breathe in through the nose, into the bottom of the lungs, the belly a dome pulling down the diaphragm; chest out; ribs out. Pause. Breathe out, squeezing air from the bottom of the lungs first: belly comes in, diaphragm goes up; chest comes down, ribs out. Pause. Repeat.

This is how we need to be breathing in silent prayer, and there's no harm in using it at other times too. It becomes habitual after a while. For now, though, it will feel artificial. That's OK. Go with it. You can probably do four of these breaths in a minute. So please do around 16 of them now, and nothing else.

4 minutes

Genesis 2.7

... then the LORD God formed a human from the dust of the ground, and breathed into his nostrils the breath of life; and the human became a living being.

Question for reflection

Does it feel strange, or familiar, to breathe into the bottom of your lungs? Could you do it all the time?

Prayer

O God
who shaped me in my mother's womb,
as I breathe your life
let me find again the peace
of the trusting child you made me to be.

Day 13

Looking at What?

We have spoken before about the differences between seeing and listening. In silent prayer our focus is on listening. Those with a visual impairment may thus have an interestingly distinctive experience of silent prayer, and perhaps even enjoy some advantages – starting a little further up the mountain than those who can see. But if you have the power of sight you have to decide what to do with it. What are we going to look at during our times of silent prayer?

I recommend looking at the eyelids from within. Eyes open, we are more prone to notice, plan, analyse. The eyes gather clues that start trains of thought, leading us into memory or hope or anxiety or ambition.

That said, it is possible to see in an attentive, receptive way that can be like listening. Moreover, we want the peaceful openness of silent prayer to permeate our whole lives with outward-focused calm, and we can't go around with our eyes shut. So why not keep our eyes open in silent prayer? Some do. You could simply gaze around in receptive calm. Some recommend concentrating on the flame of a candle. My confessor, deeply steeped in Orthodox spirituality, would think you ill-advised to gaze at anything but an icon.

Icons we should take particularly seriously. If we gaze at an icon, something yet more may be going on. The prayerfulness of the painter, the sanctity of the subject-matter, and above all the generosity of the Holy Spirit, may make our gazing on an icon something more than we can know with our eyes shut.

I am enough of an instinctive Protestant to feel it's probably not for me. In any event, using icons in prayer needs to be done properly or not at all, and ideally not in isolation from the whole religious culture of which it is a part. But icons have been part of the spiritual growth and deepening of millions of men and women for over 2,000 years, so there may be something in it for you. If you want to explore it further, take a look at the book by Vladimir Ouspensky in the Further Reading section. Or head for Mount Athos.

These explorations are for a lifetime in which you will do well to try a few experiments in what helps you go deeper. For now, however, I recommend simply closing your eyes. There are already more than enough memories, plans, hopes, regrets, shopping lists, train times, arguments and Netflix boxsets swirling around our fevered bonces. We don't need more stimulation. We don't need to think 'I must get rid of that cobweb' or 'it's clean in here, I ought to dust the bedroom'. A sound from outside already gives a new focus for listening. If our eyes are shut, we save ourselves the momentary impulse to go beyond listening into investigation.

As we go further on with listening, we shall learn ways of looking that are not this. We shall learn to gaze. We shall find ways to integrate silent prayer and moving about in daily life without bumping into doorposts. But let's make it as easy as we can for now. We increase our time again today. Please spend 5 minutes looking at the inside of your eyelids.

5 minutes

From Charles Wesley, 'O for a Heart to Praise My God'

My heart, Thou know'st, can never rest
Till Thou create my peace;
Till of mine Eden repossest,
From self, and sin, I cease.
Thy nature, gracious Lord, impart;
Come quickly from above;
Write Thy new name upon my heart,
Thy new best name of love.

Question for reflection

What do you see when you close your eyes?

Prayer

As I close my eyes in your presence, Lord,
open the eyes of my heart
and let me gaze on you
with all that I am
for all of eternity.

Day 14

When?

If you are a musician or an athlete, how often (and when) do you practise or train? Probably every day. Probably more or less the same time each day. Sometimes you take a day off, but if it is a day off the norm is to be 'on'. When you play a concert or compete, you're on somebody else's schedule. You may also play or run for sheer joy at any hour of the day and night. But the backbone of excellence is regularity.

It's the same with silent prayer. Like a lot of the things we've talked about, there's room for different practices. You may find a different way. But I recommend daily, about the same time each day.

Let me give you three reasons.

First, it's easier to keep a regular habit. A real habit is in its very nature *regular*. We benefit from the rhythm, just as you benefit from muscle memory in a movement you know well. And it's harder to wriggle out of. Without a regular time I can put it off, forget it for a day, lose count of how often a week. If it's daily at the same time, you know where you are. Inertia helps too. When the norm is to do it, *not doing* it takes choice and effort.

Second, you think about it less, which helps you to get it right. Silent prayer is paradoxical – we take hold of letting go, concentrate on not concentrating, try not to try. Letting go of intention, control and striving gets easier when we have fewer decisions to make. If your time of silent prayer is something that you are always deciding about, then the thought 'I'm about to do some silence' is front of mind. This pushes you further away from silence. If you commit to the same time, after a few months (or years or decades) you're simply there without intending to be. We'll talk about this more on Day 23.

Third, a daily routine of silent prayer builds up. I take an annual retreat at a Cistercian abbey: five days, four nights. The first year of the pandemic aside, I've gone every year since I was ordained a priest. But it's not five days a year. I don't go out of the world and do something different and then come back to 'normal'. I am in the monastery an hour every three days. I am in the monastery 1 second in 70. I am always there. The monastic rhythm is like a flywheel, always turning, lending its energy. Like a gyroscope, it helps with balance too. A daily time of silent prayer works the same way. Again, I am sharing my own experience as well as stating a general truth. When the habit is established, silence builds up in your bloodstream; silence is always there, a golden thread running through all the dramas and challenges and joys of the rest of the day. It builds up.

So I recommend you pick a time and try it. If you find it works, stick with it. Or try a different time. Pick a time that doesn't bother anyone else, when you are less likely to be interrupted, when you will be alert. When you've found the right time, stick to it.

If that's all sounding like 'first thing in the morning', then why make it more complicated? I bet it's what most people do. It works for me.

5 minutes

From Charles Wesley, 'Forth in Thy Name'

Forth in thy name, O Lord, I go,
My daily labour to pursue,
Thee, only thee, resolved to know
In all I think or speak or do.
The task thy wisdom hath assigned,
O let me cheerfully fulfil;
In all my works thy presence find,
And prove thy good and perfect will.

Question for reflection

How much or how little regularity is there in your day, how do you feel about that, and how much control do you have over this in practical terms?

Prayer

God who makes the sun to rise and set,
who makes my heart to beat,
may I find my place
in the peaceful daily pattern
of your good and ordered purposes.

Day 15

Where?

So you have chosen a time of day. You can always change it if it doesn't work, but stay with it for now and at some point simply commit to a time.

Then *where* are you going to be silent? Should you start every morning walking around the house thinking ... hmm ... in the kitchen today or the bedroom ... where do I fancy today ... which chair ... maybe outside ...?

What do you think?

Yep, you got me. To nobody's surprise I'm going to recommend the same place each day, for all the reasons we talked about. If you're going to sit (remember what we talked about on Days 9 and 10), you want to sit well. That means the right chair, and when you get a chair that works you don't want to be lugging it from room to room. And the points in favour of the same time are also points in favour of the same place. It makes the habit easier to keep. It's one less thing to think about. It helps the daily pattern seep into all of you, wherever, whenever.

Silent prayer is serious work. Does a mechanic or a carpenter fix a motorcycle or make a table in a different room each day? If you drive and own a car, think of the difference between getting into your car and driving off versus getting into a hire car for the first time.

Of course, we are allowed to enter into silent prayer anywhere at any time. One of the joys is that it's portable. Soon we shall talk about taking silence on to the streets and integrating it into the whole of our lives. But first we need the hard core of disciplined practice that resources and deepens everything else. This is best done in the same place every day.

And you know what? You can make that one place really lovely. Pick the corner or the window or wherever is going to be your place, and putting your chair there can be the start of a project. You may choose austerity: week to week you can declutter your eyeline, remove ornaments, straighten curtains. Or you may want beauty. Try a plant, or a vase. But make your choice comfortable. A beautiful rug for the knees on chilly mornings. Just the right cushion. (But remember, not *too* comfortable.)

This is your workshop: make it work.

Wait, though, for Days 25–27 before you go nap on a room because I have another suggestion.

Now it's time for 5 more minutes of silence. You've got the fundamentals, and the fundamentals are all you need. That, and practice. Tomorrow we will start on aspects of this that are harder – indeed impossible – to grasp. But today we are at the end of the beginning so I wanted to ask how it's going. Has there been a day when you have thought 'don't much fancy it'? And did you do it anyway? So, well done. Growth comes through perseverance. The days when perseverance is costly are days when real growth comes. Keep on keeping on.

5 minutes

Psalm 84

How lovely is your dwelling place
O Lord of hosts!
My soul longs, indeed it faints
for the courts of the Lord;
my heart and my flesh sing for joy
to the living God.
Even the sparrow finds a home,
and the swallow a nest for herself,
where she may lay her young,
at your altars, O Lord of hosts,
my King and my God.
Happy are those who live in your house,
ever singing your praise.

Question for reflection

Where do you feel most at peace?

Prayer

Lord Jesus,
as you had nowhere to lay your head,
I have no home but heaven,
no shelter but the tent of pilgrimage:
but when you provide,
for a day, a year or a lifetime,
somewhere safe and beautiful to sit,
may I sit there with you.

Day 16

Dostoevsky's Polar Bear

Fyodor Dostoevsky would probably say true silent prayer is particularly hard for *us*. By 'us' I mean people with what Dostoevsky calls the 'Western personality'. That may not be you. But, for good or ill, it sure is me. I think most readers will say likewise. If the cap fits ...

Dostoevsky says the 'Western personality' 'fights for what it wants; it demands its rights; it desires to separate' (Dostoevsky, *Winter Notes on Summer Impressions*, p. 111). He thinks it would take a thousand years for us to renounce our false individuality and attain the true individual freedom that can give itself entirely to others.

He is writing about society and politics, but the problem he puts his finger on is a problem for silent prayer. And silent prayer probably does flourish in the Eastern churches in a way it does not in the Catholic and Protestant West where the habit of self-forgetfulness is not so strong.

Dostoevsky says the 'Western personality' is like someone 'trying not to think of a polar bear' (Dostoevsky, *Winter Notes on Summer Impressions*, pp. 112).

Try it. Try not thinking of a polar bear. Go on.

You see the problem? The moment you achieved success and congratulated yourself on not thinking of a ... oops, now you're thinking of a polar bear.

Faced with a challenge or a possibility to realize, our go-to is to *do* something; and when we have done it, perhaps to pat ourselves on the back. In many ways this is great. It makes for an energetic, productive, wealthy society. But it doesn't help us with silent prayer. For silent prayer is not about doing, and it's not about me. You notice we have not spoken of 'praying silently' but of 'entering into silent prayer'? For silent prayer is not something you do. But, then, what *are* you going to do?

This has to unfold. It may be hard for us if we do have the 'Western personality', but I don't think anyone finds it easy. Tibetan Buddhists have to work at it, and if anyone doesn't have the 'Western personality' it would be a Tibetan Buddhist. Either way, we start where we start, and as we go on in these 40 days we shall find some ways not to *do* silent prayer but gently to stop *not* doing it.

From now on, though, we are in the world of paradox and mystery. So far we have dealt with things you can see and touch: why silent prayer is good for us, the physical realities of how, where and when we sit and breathe. Now we have to get to grips with this central challenge of true silent prayer.

The 'silence' of silent prayer is not just the absence of vibrating air. We do not enter into silent prayer by going into a quiet room and not speaking out loud. We *can* do that and it may help us, but doing it does not constitute silent prayer. Silent prayer is at its heart a silencing of the self, and silencing the self is like trying not to think of a polar bear. If this all sounds mysterious and hard to grasp, good. For it is no more about grasping than it is about doing. It is, however, supremely worthwhile *not* doing and *not* grasping.

Let me leave the last word to Dostoevsky: 'What is to be done then? Well, there is nothing you can do about it; rather it must happen of itself; it must be present in one's nature' (Dostoevsky, *Winter Notes on Summer Impressions*).

So now, do nothing about it for another 5 minutes please.

5 minutes

St Augustine

A remark attributed by many (but by none whom I have read precisely) to St Augustine – to be fair, it is the sort of thing he would have said even if he didn't:

> *Si comprehendis, non est Deus*
> or, in English, 'if you have understood it, it is not God'

Question for reflection

Can you not think of a polar bear?

Prayer

O God,
you are utterly beyond,
yet you make yourself known:
as I cry out to you,
let me hear more than my own voice;
as I seek you,
let not my seeking be all that I find.

Day 17

Be Here Now

From now on we are going to meet resistance, for we are in the territory of Dostoevsky's polar bear – the territory of paradox and oxymoron.

We are being purposeful about renouncing our purposes.
We are thinking about not thinking.
We are holding fast to letting go.
We are trying not to try.

When we do it, we are not doing it. When we succeed, we fail. When we think it's working, it's not working. This is going to take a while. It's going to take eternity.

Be of good courage! The higher up the mountain we climb, the higher we see the mountain is, and we never get to the top. But to be on the journey is to arrive. The journey into silent prayer is a journey into God. Jesus, God with us, says 'I am the way'. If we are on the way, we are at the end. It sounds paradoxical. That's OK. Others have trod this way before us. Simply start wherever and whenever you are.

And where are you? When are you?

Here, now.

That's it. Start here, now. Be here, now. Then we are already on our way. More, if we really are here, now, we are also at our journey's end.

Let's not make this more mysterious than it is. Be here. What is here? Your breath is here. We have already learned to sense the breath. Lean into that. The muscles that extend and contract the lungs, the feeling of air flowing in and out, the gentle sighing sound as air passes through the nose. What else is here? Maybe your body is making little noises. Listen to them. There may be sounds from the street outside. They are here. Attend. Don't analyse or recognize. Welcome them. There is a wider world with thousands of streets, millions of homes, billions of stars, but it's in God's hands and it will be there when you need it. Let it go for now. No imagining. No travelling in the mind. Just let what is here expand to fill the space. Above all, listen. Listen to what is here. Don't imagine what might be here or remember what isn't here. Listen to what is here. Be here.

And more: be here, now.

Again, this won't come easily. Living in past and future is part of the human condition. And that's a good thing: to be fully human is to be responsible for, and learn from, the past and to live purposefully into the future. Yet God is in eternity, not in linear time with past and future. God is always here, now – for ever. In silent prayer we hope to enter God's reality. That means being fully present now. Not 'living for the moment'. Very much the reverse in fact. We do not abandon responsibility for past and future. We become more truly continuous with our past and future selves. But this comes as we inhabit the one eternal moment of God's presence, free from regret for what has gone, and anxiety for what will come. This is eternal life: not only living for ever, but living in eternity right here, right now.

Again it's paradoxical. Remember not to remember, plan to make no plans. I never told you this was going to be easy … but persevere. Be now. Not a few seconds ago. Not anticipating the next breath. Now. Here. Take 6 minutes to be here, now. And know this: whatever else is here, now, God is always here, now.

6 minutes

From John Ernest Bode, 'O Jesus, I have promised'

O let me hear Thee speaking
in accents clear and still,
above the storms of passion,
the murmurs of self-will;
O speak to reassure me,
to hasten or control!
O speak, and make me listen,
Thou Guardian of my soul!

Question for reflection

When your attention wanders from the immediate present, does it tend to wander to the past or to the future?

Prayer

Spirit of truth and peace,
be in me the mysterious power
to let go of letting go,
not to seek, but to find.

Day 18

The End of the Beginning

We are almost halfway through now. Does silent prayer feel different from when you started? Is it more familiar? Or more deeply mysterious? Or both? Pause and remember.

Let's sum up where we've got to.

We saw how countercultural silent prayer is. Not the technological acquisitiveness of seeing, but an open listening presence. It opens up depths and this can be daunting. We saw how hard, but how necessary, it is to find silence in this world where so many people and businesses are trying to feed our dopamine system and lure us into consuming and producing.

We learned to sit up, alert but not tense, comfortable but not slumped, rooted on the ground, weight spread evenly, hands together, forearms on thighs, using core strength to sit in balance. We learnt to breathe by filling our lungs from the bottom, pushing out the abdomen, then the sternum, then the ribs. To breathe out by squeezing the lungs from the bottom as though squeezing the air out of an airbed.

We determined to listen and to be here, now. And we noticed that this is paradoxical. For the more we strive to let go of elsewhere, of past and present, the more they come to our attention. But we persevere. We go on being here, now, knowing that whatever is here, now, God is always here, now.

At this point you could put the book away.

By now you see two things are true. First, all there is to it is sitting, breathing and listening, here, now. Second, there are depths to this simple business that we will never fathom.

There is really no better way to go on, then, than build up to 10 minutes a day and stick at it. Sitting and breathing:

listening, here, now. There's no clever trick. No higher arcana. No access code. The whole of eternity is there in a nutshell. Sitting, breathing and listening, here, now. There is always a yet more, always a depth beyond depth. Our journey into God never ends. Yet on the way we are already at our journey's end.

Nevertheless, I feel responsible. True, I am no adept or grandmaster. Heaven forfend! Silent prayer is not something we master: it is letting go of mastery. But I'm really not a master. I'm a beginner. If I am a little further up the mountain, it's only by a few switchbacks, and the mountain is infinitely high. All the same, I want to walk with you another three or four weeks so when you go on alone you have a steadier pace and more of a spring in your step. I want to tell you a few things I have found on the mountain so far.

In the remaining days we go more into things you can *do* to deepen this paradoxical habit that is about *not doing*. Then we will talk about silent prayer with other people, and how to go beyond 10 minutes a day of intentional silence and infuse the whole of life with listening (and let this feed back to deepen our silence). At the end we link it up with theology. With whom do we keep silence? To whom do we listen?

But please hold to this simple deep truth: it's just sitting, breathing and listening, here, now. Please now take another 6 minutes to listen, sitting and breathing, here, now.

6 minutes

From Maria Willis, 'Father, Hear the Prayer We Offer'

Not for ever in green pastures
do we ask our way to be;
but the steep and rugged pathway
may we tread rejoicingly.
Not for ever by still waters
would we idly rest and stay;
but would smite the living fountains
from the rocks along our way.

Question for reflection

Think back to Day 1 – what has changed in your outlook on silent prayer?

Prayer

Lord Jesus
you walked mile after mile with your disciples,
you fasted in the desert,
you sat for hours on the cold mountain top:
help me to keep on climbing towards you,
be the way that I tread,
and walk with me.

Day 19

A Body Scan

Now try this. We are going to work our way up the body, attending to each segment during the time it takes to breathe in and out three times. Please read this and fix it in your mind, then put the book away, sit and breathe, eyes shut, listening. Then do this:

1. Attend to your feet and ankles. Are your feet hot or cold? Dry or damp? Any pains or itches? Any pressure from floor or shoe? How are your ankles? While noticing all this, take three of your usual good, slow, deep breaths.
2. Attend to your legs from the ankle to the knee. Are your knees sore or strong? If they feel sore, are they actually sore now, or are you (if you're my age) simply conscious that they are often sore? Are your calves warm or cool? Strong or weak? Take three breaths and be aware of this segment of your legs.
3. Attend to the legs from knee to pelvis. Are your thighs tired or refreshed? Any pressure points under your bottom? Wriggle to distribute your weight evenly. Breathe three times, fully aware of the longest bones and largest muscles in your body.
4. Attend to your pelvis and lower back. Is your pelvis rocked forward to balance you over your thighs? Feel the pelvis as a great hinge between the legs that move and the torso, whose job is to stay still and hold everything together. How is your lower back? Is your lower spine curved or straight? Ideally, it is straight. Is this another area of aches

and pains? Are they real or anticipated? Pay attention to how it feels now. Take three more breaths.

5 Attend to your upper back. Is it curved or straight? Tense or relaxed? If it's tense, drop the shoulders a little. But mainly just be aware of how it is. Take three more breaths.

6 Now we start again at the far end of the arms. Attend to your hands. Hot or cold, dry or damp? Skin rough or smooth? Be aware of each finger. Take three more breaths.

7 Attend to your forearms. Are they resting comfortably? How do they feel? Notice your elbows. Be aware of both bones inside each forearm as you take three more breaths.

8 Attend to your upper arms. Are they hanging loosely? Or tense? Warm or cool? Be aware of them as you take three breaths.

9 Attend to your shoulders and neck. Is there tension or a feeling of relaxation? You have come now to the junction between the path upwards from the feet and the path upwards from the hands. Be aware of how everything comes together here. Feel the weight of your head on your neck as you take three breaths.

10 Attend to your eyes, mouth and nose. Simply acknowledge the eyes (again this will be different for the visually impaired), then experience three breaths entering and leaving the body.

11 Attend to your skull and scalp. How does your head feel? Do various parts feel different, or are they all the same? You have a brain that you are using to experience other things: experience your brain and its container for three breaths.

12 Attend to your ears. Are they warm or cool? They have been hearing all this time. Now attend to them. Let their hearing become listening.

Depending on how fast you breathe, this takes 4 or 5 minutes. At the end, carry on listening for a minute or two.

6 minutes

Psalm 139.12–16

For you yourself created my inmost parts;
you knit me together in my mother's womb.
I thank you, for I am fearfully and wonderfully made;
marvellous are your works, my soul knows well.
My frame was not hidden from you,
when I was made in secret
and woven in the depths of the earth.
Your eyes beheld my form, as yet unfinished;
already in your book were all my members written,
As day by day they were fashioned
when as yet there was none of them.

Question for reflection

What if anything has changed in your sense of your body, and the body's integration with the whole person, since we learned to sit and breathe?

Prayer

Creator God,
thank you for the blood in my veins,
the air in my lungs,
the marrow in my bones:
thank you for making me
for life in all its fullness.

Day 20

Something to Do

What was all that about yesterday?

Many traditions recommend something like a 'body scan' and it is popular in the secular world of 'mindfulness'. But it is something we *do*, and surely *doing* is not what we are about?

The challenge in silent prayer is to let go of intention, action and effort when our go-to way of meeting a challenge is to make intentional active effort. So we need things to *do* that do not confine us to further *doing* by setting off trains of thought or posing puzzles to solve. We need something to do that we swim through, that doesn't catch us like kelp round our ankles but lets us float up towards the light of true silent listening prayer.

A body scan can be this. Of the many purposeful things we can do it is among the least like purposeful doing. It's not in itself silent prayer. But it is a lot more like silence than thinking through your holiday plans or worrying about which car insurance to buy or trying to remember the name of the sister of that guy from work. So it can be a way in. When we find ourselves needing to do *something*, we can opt to do this and it will at least not lead us to further *doing*.

A body scan can help us be here, now. For, of course, the body is always here, now. Your bones are always here, now. Your blood is always here, now. Your legs and arms and back and head are always here, now. Moreover, a body scan paced by your breathing keeps focus on the breath in a helpful way.

I suggest you make this part of your time of silence every day for the next few days – longer if you like, but at least long enough that you get a feel for it. Then keep it handy for a day when you don't settle and your mind is active, puzzling, worrying, remembering. A day when you are more than usually prone to *doing*. When that day comes, do a body scan.

Again there's nothing particularly clever here. There are lots of different ways to do it. The internet will furnish you with alternatives if you don't get on with my system. The thing is to pick one way and go with it. Have it ready to hand when you need it.

One long-term payoff from the body scan is a more integrated awareness of the body, so we become more at ease with our bodies. The body is a large part of what is here, now. It is not something to compare with the past or other people or some abstract ideal. And I am of course aware that not every reader has two legs, two feet, two arms and two hands. Those who do not may have some extra exploration to do – whether to focus on what isn't there, as well as what is, for instance. But really, every body is unique. We have all changed shape over our lives and each of us needs to find our own way to scan our own distinctive body.

Over time, as you become more and more aware of your body, here, now, you may find that simply attending to the whole body for a moment is enough to ground you. Yet it will always be helpful to come back to the full body scan now and then, so you don't lose touch.

Now, another body scan as the focus of your next 6 minutes of listening silence, here, now.

6 minutes

From George Eliot, *Adam Bede*, chapter 29

Our deeds determine us, as much as we determine our deeds, and until we know what has been or will be the peculiar combination of outward with inward facts, which constitutes a man's critical actions, it will be better not to think ourselves wise about his character. There is a terrible coercion in our deeds ...

Question for reflection

What do you find helps you to be grounded and still?

Prayer

God our father,
from everlasting
to everlasting,
you are:
help me from day to day
to be.

Day 21

Something to Say

As we become more still, put aside work, sit down, stop fidgeting, calm our breath, words will be the last thing we let go of. Words have ingenious energy to draw us away from listening silence. Maybe we will always have words in our minds, until beyond this mortal life we see face to face and know ourselves as we are fully known. Certainly words will be present in our listening silence for a good while to come, so we had better have some good words.

We need to find a few words or phrases that centre us and lead us up towards the light. They need to become habitual so they come to mind when we need them, displacing words that are trivial or distracting.

Here's a good word start you off:

'Listen.'

If you can get so you automatically hear 'Listen' in your mind's ear, gently with weight, it will cue other good habits of being here, now, breathing, sitting right, letting go. A loving, authoritative reminder.

'Listen.'

And remember it's not just you saying this. Wise saints repeat the word down the ages. Let us hear them. And more: if with integrity we can hear this as God's word, then we are really on the way.

'Listen.'

Then have a few longer phrases to hand. Not many. They need to become familiar through use, so they fit your mind as the wooden-handed trowel fits into the hand of the gardener who has dug with it for 40 years. They need to become words that say themselves. Choose well and few.

You may have a favourite poem, hymn or worship song that speaks of listening and silence. I love this prayer of Walter Hilton, a medieval mystic:

'I am nothing, I have nothing, I desire nothing but the love of Jesus' (Hilton, *The Ladder of Perfection*, p. 159).

Try it with the breath. Inhale the familiar three stages cued by the three 'I's. Then exhale on 'but the love of Jesus'.

Above all, turn to the Scriptures. The point of our listening is to hear God. If the words that come to mind are words of Scripture, then we are on the right path. Perhaps you can think of some verses that speak of silence, listening, depth.

'On God alone my soul in stillness waits' (Ps. 62.1).

'In the morning, while it was still very dark, he got up and went out to a deserted place, and there he prayed' (Mark. 1.35).

'[The] Spirit intercedes with sighs too deep for words' (Rom. 8.26).

For me, it's 1 Samuel 3.9 and Psalm 46.10.

At the start of a time of silence, as the boy Samuel said when he heard God calling in the Temple: 'Speak, for your servant is listening.'

When the body scan comes to an end: 'Speak, for your servant is listening.'

When, as so often, the mind wanders: 'Speak, for your servant is listening.'

Then if I am in a place where – without fooling myself or faking it – I can hear words of Scripture as spoken by God I open my mind to Psalm 46. I say in my mind – or do I perhaps hear it in my mind? – the words of God spoken through the Psalmist: 'be still, and know that I am God'.

Sometimes it is a dialogue. And if it really is a dialogue, then that is almost enough:

'Speak, for your servant is listening.'

'Be still, and know that I am God.'

Today we increase our time of silence to 7 minutes.

7 minutes

James 3.9–12

With the tongue we bless the Lord and Father, and with it we curse those who are made in the likeness of God. From the same mouth come blessing and cursing. My brothers and sisters, this ought not to be so. Does a spring pour forth from the same opening both fresh and brackish water? Can a fig tree, my brothers and sisters, yield olives, or a grapevine figs? No more can salt water yield fresh.

Question for reflection

Are there words or phrases so familiar to you that they come to mind without conscious thought, and are they good words?

Prayer

Father God,
who sent your son into the world
to give us true life:
teach me the words
that will lead me to the Word.

Day 22

Pole Vaulting in Zero G

Now we are up to 7 minutes a day and I hope you are still doing the body scan every day for the time being. See if it brings you to a state of simply listening, here, now, present, alert and aware, but not active. If it does, though, in all likelihood it will only be for fleeting moments. You are, after all, at the start of this journey.

It is said that when Archbishop Michael Ramsey was asked in a radio interview how long he prayed each day, he replied 'About a minute.'

'Shouldn't we worry, Archbishop, that the leader of the Established Church only spends a minute a day saying his prayers?' the interviewer asked.

'Oh no, you misunderstand me. I spend more than an hour a day "saying my prayers". I only spend a minute praying.'

We long for a perfect open presence before God, wholly receptive, listening, here, now. Maybe some saints inhabit this state for hours at a time, for a whole lifetime. For most of us, if we do find that place of attentive silent openness to God, we should be glad if it lasts even as long as that one minute Archbishop Michael knew.

Think of it like weightlessness and balance.

We are not astronauts on the space station, so we are not going to be weightless all the time. But if we get on a swing and really get it going so we swing through an arc of 180 degrees, at the end of each arc – when we are facing directly down to Earth or on our backs looking up at the stars, when our upward motion stops and we start to go back down – there is one infinitesimal moment when we are neither ascending nor descending. We are weightless. You get the same thing on a trampoline – and for rather longer if you fly an aeroplane in a ballistic arc and cut the motors. Between rising and falling: weightlessness.

Or think of a pole vaulter. Nobody could balance on top of a 5-metre carbonfibre pole indefinitely. But pole vaulters, even the most unsuccessful ones who never clear the bar, all balance on top of their poles for one unmeasurable moment, one infinitely small segment of their vault. Again, it's not a tenable position. But it is a moment of balance.

It may be in similar moments that we are able to pass through the mysterious weightless balance of true silence: 'At the still point of the turning world … there the dance is, but neither arrest nor movement' (Eliot, *Four Quartets*, p. 5).

Let's try it now. Let's try it with the breath.

Seven minutes. Start with the body scan. Then when you have worked your way up to the listening ears, simply breathe and listen, here, now. But be attentive at the moment when breathing in has ceased and breathing out has not yet begun; and again when the lungs are empty and you have not yet started to fill them.

Unlike the top of the swing or the vault, you have some control over the length of this moment. Don't prolong it too much to start with. When you are able to be in that moment (bear in mind that though this may come naturally, it might also take months of practice), stretch it for a second or two. But for now just let yourself be weightless, balanced and silent right there at the top of the vault, in the instant of weightlessness between breathing in and breathing out.

7 minutes

Arthur Schnabel, Pianist (in the *Chicago Daily News*, 11 June 1958)

The notes I handle no better than many pianists. But the pauses between the notes – ah, that is where the art resides!

Question for reflection

How long can you pause your thoughts before they start again?

Prayer

God of grace,
from the earth
on which you have placed me
I leap as high as I can;
before I sink again,
reach down from your infinite height
and touch my outstretched hand.

Day 23

Groundhog Mountaineering

However we approach it, it's the same problem. We have good words that come to mind, but we don't want them to cling to us. We shrug with a forgiving smile when the mind wanders. We focus on the breath. But they are all things to do, and of course we strive to cease doing. This is not going to stop being a problem.

We do improve. It takes time, but that time passes. We are never the best, but we get better and better. And as we tread the long road to good silence, we are always at least on the edge of good silence. Those tiny slivers of moments between one thought and another when there is real listening are valuable and life-giving.

Nevertheless, we need to keep moving on upwards day by day, making the same mistakes, but at least making them quicker so we can get on to making new mistakes.

Have you seen *Groundhog Day*? Bill Murray is doomed to live the same day again and again until he gets it right. The same conceit comes up in a few other movies. In *The Edge of Tomorrow*, Tom Cruise fights his way up the same alien-infested beach again and again, each time a little farther as he dodges the ever more familiar hazards. In *Source Code*, Jake Gyllenhaal fails to thwart the same bomber again and again until he gets it right. It's a great premise for a movie: the chance to learn from our mistakes.

The early high-altitude mountaineers climbed the great Himalayan peaks by the 'siege' technique. Relays of mountaineers climbed, fixed ropes, left stores, descended, then climbed the fixed ropes, ate the stores, and climbed higher, leaving more fixed ropes and more stores. By the time the summit party was on its way, everyone had climbed the bottom pitches so many times that what had been a daunting unknown wilderness was now a well-worn path up which they scampered without a thought.

This is a big part of why we go for regularity in silent prayer.

We want the challenges and distractions to become familiar and the ways to get past them to be second nature. We go round and round the same here and now, each time meeting the same resistance, each time overcoming resistance the same way, each time with greater fluidity. The strange rocky path becomes our path. We know it with our eyes closed. Obstacles become old friends to be patted gently as we pass on.

The mind wanders in the same old way and is brought back to the centre in the same old way – each time a little quicker, a little more gently. Those Bible verses we chose that bring us back to the centre, that lift our eyes from the detail of our hopes and worries to the simple immensity of heaven: day by day they come more easily and naturally. That tiny shard of a moment between breathing in and breathing out when you are poised in the eternal moment of listening silence: each time you encounter that moment, you can balance in it a little longer.

We climb the same mountain every day. Each day our moves are smoother, the holds easier to find. Each day we are quicker up the lower pitches. Each day, we go higher up the mountain.

7 minutes

Christina Rossetti, 'Up-hill'

Does the road wind up-hill all the way?
   Yes, to the very end.
Will the day's journey take the whole long day?
   From morn to night, my friend.

But is there for the night a resting-place?
   A roof for when the slow dark hours begin.
May not the darkness hide it from my face?
   You cannot miss that inn.

Shall I meet other wayfarers at night?
   Those who have gone before.
Then must I knock, or call when just in sight?
   They will not keep you standing at that door.

Shall I find comfort, travel-sore and weak?
   Of labour you shall find the sum.
Will there be beds for me and all who seek?
   Yea, beds for all who come.

Question for reflection

What simple, practical things can you do that will make it easier for you to enter into silent prayer?

Prayer

Father God,
you came from the infinite beyond
to live among us in your son:
I long to ascend nearer
to the heights where you dwell;
help me to learn the path
day by day.

Day 24

Puppies, Ripples and Toddlers

Our minds are energetic and curious, always jumping up and frisking about and darting down rabbit holes, following a scent, digging things out. The smallest sight or sound sets them off. Usually it's nothing significant, but one thought leads to another. We are like a puppy chasing a tennis ball, nudging it to keep it rolling.

You sit, silent, attentive. But something occurs ... what you need at the shops ... that thing on TV last night ... a challenging conversation ... the new job ... where did I put the keys? This is going to keep happening.

Even when you've been at this for years, you are still going to have to wait for it to pass.

On a windless day you cast a stone into the middle of a still pond. Concentric circles of ripples spread to the edge. Some energy dissipates as they push mud or sand up the shore, but most of it goes into a new ripple going back to the middle of the pond. On the way, it meets other returning ripples. They bounce off each other. Soon the pond is a grid of ripples, an untidy tartan, smaller ripples but more of them. In time it becomes an evenly stippled surface like pebbledash. But it will be a long time before the pond returns to mirror-like calm.

When your mind wanders, you have to wait for it to pass – only you have to wait it out in a way that doesn't make more ripples. Don't rush down to the edge of the pond and beat the ripples with a tree branch. Sit it out.

If you have ever taken a toddler into an antique shop, you know all about this. The moment you realize this was a bad idea comes too late. Independent locomotion is a new discovery for your young companion, which they are exploring to the full, almost afraid the gift will be withdrawn. And here are many intriguing objects to handle. They don't know these objects are fragile – or if they *do* know, that is a further source of delight. And now they're 2 metres ahead of you and moving fast. It's new. It's a game. It's exciting.

If you are going to save the situation you need to be careful what energy you bring to it. Young children imitate. If you chase your young companion, that will simply provide additional excitement by turning this game into a game of 'chase'. But you have to do something or there will be scratched escritoires. So you squat. You make your voice low and mellow but audible. 'Hey, youngster' – eye contact, a calm smile, open hands – 'wanna come over here?'

The mind wanders in silent prayer. If we rebuke it and try to wrestle it back into line, that is simply another form of the wandering mind. If you force yourself to be silent, the forcing breaks the silence. No bold leap will free us from the wandering mind, for a bold leap is always a leap away from true silence. Berating yourself for 'getting it wrong' does not make for peaceful listening: when we berate ourselves, we draw attention to the thing we are 'doing wrong' and are thus more likely to do it again.

Instead, we treat our thoughts like wayward toddlers. They are good and lovable – but just a little bit unruly. So a shrug, a gentle smile (we will see on Day 30 the strange power of smiling), and a nod with a raised eyebrow towards the better path.

Love; forgive; sit, breathe; be here, now; listen. For as long as it takes.

7 minutes

From Lewis Carroll, *Through the Looking-glass*

'I should see the garden far better,' said Alice to herself, 'if I could get to the top of that hill: and here's a path that leads straight to it – at least, no, it doesn't do that ... It's more like a corkscrew than a path! ... This goes straight back to the house! Well then, I'll try it the other way ... It's no use talking about it,' Alice said, looking up at the house and pretending it was arguing with her. 'I'm not going in again yet ...'

So, resolutely turning her back upon the house, she set out once more down the path ... she was just saying, 'I really shall do it this time –' when the path gave a sudden twist and shook itself (as she described it afterwards), and the next moment she found herself actually walking in at the door ...

'You can't possibly do that,' said the Rose: 'I should advise you to walk the other way.'

This sounded nonsense to Alice, so she said nothing, but set off at once towards the Red Queen. To her surprise, she lost sight of her in a moment, and found herself walking in at the front-door again. A little provoked, she drew back, and after looking everywhere ... thought she would try the plan, this time, of walking in the opposite direction.

It succeeded beautifully. She had not been walking a minute before she found herself face to face ... full in sight of the hill she had been so long aiming at.

Question for reflection

Can you think of other things that you can't get by chasing or grasping them?

Prayer

Lord Jesus,
you took the nature of a slave,
obedient to death,
and received the name
above all names:
help me to live the truth
that only by letting go of my life
will I truly live.

Day 25

Other People

If you want to join me for silent prayer it's simple: 8.45–8.55am, the east end of the bench on the north side of the Lady Chapel at Holy Trinity Church, Roehampton. Every day except Saturday.

This has the advantages we talked about. It's a regular time and place. The bench is the right height and bottom-shaped but made of hard wood, so a balance between comfortable and alert. The space is beautiful. Two candles on the stone altar. Behind, in a semi-circle stand, are the matriarchs of Jesus' extended family: Elizabeth, Mary and Anne in stained glass. Above, the blue ceiling is painted with silver stars and a rising sun. It can be chilly in winter but I have the perfect puffy coat with a slightly monastic hood.

One thing is different from all that we've talked about so far. There are other people there. Always at least one, sometimes half a dozen. Morning Prayer in Roehampton is 8.30. The bell rings at 8.25, though I may not stumble over from the vicarage before 8.29. Pray. Say the psalms. Read the Old Testament. Say a canticle. Read the New Testament. Say the responsory. And then, before the Benedictus, silence.

Up to now we have spoken of silence as solitary. I hope it often will be. It needs to permeate your day and opportunities for silence often arise when you are alone. Moreover, there are times when you simply need to get away and pray alone as Jesus himself often did. But if you can share your daily discipline with others, you may find this helpful and good.

You may not take to it immediately and I would be with you on that. My own fallen instinct is to avoid other people with their breathing and their eccentricities, no worse than my own but not my own, and their baffling presence, sort of like me but also so different. That's where I start. And now I'm going to tell you the truth that it is deeply life-giving to share a rhythm of silent prayer with other people. In part, this is simply because it deepens regularity. The presence of others reminds us to be present ourselves. Athletes often have training partners for similar reasons.

In the next few days we shall explore some profound things that can come out of sharing silent prayer.

Could you find or start a group? It may call for effort and ingenuity. Does your parish church have a daily time of prayer? If not, could you get something going? Could silence be part of that? Or get together with friends. If you live with other people, suggest it. If that doesn't work, you may be thinking Zoom – though I would counsel against it. Being here, now, means being *here*. If your *here* is somebody else's *there*, one of you is going to have to travel.

Then you will have to agree on how you pray together. If in doubt, use *Common Worship Daily Prayer*. Many other good liturgies are available – or make up your own pattern, so long as it has a regular pattern, with time to say the psalms and to be silent. Within those limits, find what is right for you.

This is a thing to get right in the long term, but maybe not right now. But keep it in mind. I hope one outcome of this book will be that more small communities come together to say (or even better sing) Morning and Evening Prayer. For we never forget that silence is not a zero-sum game. We are praying. God is involved. There is power here. And then we remember what Jesus said: 'where two or three are gathered in my name, I am there among them' (Matt. 18.20).

8 minutes

1 Samuel 3.4–10

Then the Lord called, 'Samuel! Samuel!' and he said, 'Here I am!' and ran to Eli, and said, 'Here I am, for you called me.' But he said, 'I did not call; lie down again.' So he went and lay down. The Lord called again, 'Samuel!' Samuel got up and went to Eli, and said, 'Here I am, for you called me.' But he said, 'I did not call, my son; lie down again.' Now Samuel did not yet know the Lord, and the word of the Lord had not yet been revealed to him. The Lord called Samuel again, a third time. And he got up and went to Eli, and said, 'Here I am, for you called me.' Then Eli perceived that the Lord was calling the boy. Therefore Eli said to Samuel, 'Go, lie down; and if he calls you, you shall say, "Speak, Lord, for your servant is listening."' So Samuel went and lay down in his place.

Now the Lord came and stood there, calling as before, 'Samuel! Samuel!' And Samuel said, 'Speak, for your servant is listening.'

Question for reflection

If your life depended on praying daily with a small group of like-minded people, what practical steps would you take to become part of such a group?

Prayer

Lord Jesus,
when you ascended
you left behind a group of friends:
thank you that when two or three of us
come together in your name
you are with us;
may we know your love for us
in our love for one another.

Day 26

Listening in the Psalms

As I mentioned earlier, every year I live with the monks at a Cistercian abbey for four days. These are men for whom spiritual discipline is a way of life. It is a hard life in many ways but a full one. And the golden thread running through it is what Benedict called 'the work of God' (Benedict, p. 10). Seven times a day, starting at 3.30am, we gather to sing the psalms.

The Book of Psalms is a compendium of 150 songs about every aspect of human life and our life with God. But there is more to the psalms than words and wisdom. A wise Californian nun once said, 'when I read the psalms, I attend to the words – but, you know, it's the rhythm, baby.'

Let me talk you through how this works.

The psalms are often published separately from the rest of the Bible, arranged as a 'psalter' for use in shared prayer. *Common Worship Daily Prayer* includes an excellent psalter – do get a copy. You will see that each verse has a break in the middle marked with a ♦. At this point, we breathe in together. And the key to making this wonderful is you breathe, but don't come to a stop. Pause: don't stop. You achieve this by keeping your pitch up at the end of the first half verse.

This is worth getting right. It may be obvious, but in case it's not, try this.

First, say out loud, in an even conversational tone,

I will exalt you, O Lord, because you have raised me up and have not let my foes triumph over me.

Did your voice stay at the same pitch throughout, only dropping to a lower pitch just before the full stop? If so, good.

Now try it again. But this time it's harder because I have laid out the text as the first verse of Psalm 30. What I want you to do is say it in exactly the same way as you did before:

I will exalt you, O Lord, because you have raised me up and have not let my foes triumph over me.

And now, still harder, here it is with the diamond halfway through. I want you to pause for breath there: otherwise, exactly as before. No dropping the pitch. Hold the tension.

I will exalt you, O Lord, because you have raised me up ♦ *and have not let my foes triumph over me.*

This may take practice, but getting it right creates an expectant silence when you are attentive, ready for what comes next. In that moment take one good breath from the bottom of the lungs.

If you go one step further and learn to sing the psalms, the shape of the music reinforces this moment of poise. But if we simply learn to say them right, the rhythm of the psalms blesses us at each verse with a moment of listening, the point of balance at the top of the pole vault.

This is wonderful to do on your own, but it is richer still with at least three like-minded people.

Divide into two groups facing each other. Take it in turns to say the verses. All pause for breath at the diamond. When your group is saying a verse, pause and breathe in; breathe out through the second half of the verse; then it's the other group's turn, and while they say the first half verse, you continue to breathe out; then you all breathe in together. And on you go.

Use that pause when you all breathe in together to lean into silent, self-forgetting listening. If nowhere else, that poised breath can be when we are truly silent, attentive, here, now.

Tomorrow we go one step further and learn to listen beyond.

8 minutes

Psalm 62

On God alone my soul in stillness waits;
from him comes my salvation.
He alone is my rock and my salvation,
my stronghold, so that I shall never be shaken.

Question for reflection

How does it change your appreciation of the psalms if you attend not only to the meaning but also to the rhythm?

Prayer

Thank you for the psalms:
For the words, for the rhythm.
As we use these words together
May we hear one another;
As we listen beyond ourselves
May we come to hear you.

Day 27

Listening Beyond

For this you really do need other people. As I said, it may take work to set up a morning prayer community. But let's say you've got your group. You have agreed on a shape for your time together and got used to it. You have learned to say the psalms at an even pace. You are keeping your pitch up in that pause for breath at mid-verse, creating that moment of anticipation: a zero-G moment at the top of the arc, a moment of listening silence.

Good.

Now here's the first thing to do.

Listen.

Listen to the others when they speak. When the other side is saying their verse, don't read the text in your book. Cover it with a card or look away. Listen to the words. Listen. To. Each. Word.

And more. When it is your turn to say a verse, listen to the people next to you as they say the words you say. Don't fall silent for they need to be able to listen to you too. But direct your hearing outwards. Hear the words you are saying said by someone else.

This can be particularly powerful if, as well as rotating through psalms over a month or two, you also use some psalms, or psalm-like texts, every day. The obvious ones are the Song of Zechariah (Luke 1.68–79) and the Song of Mary (Luke 1.46–55) which traditionally conclude Morning Prayer and Evening Prayer. Soon you will know the words. They become your words and you put the book aside. And as you speak words from your own heart, you hear those words spoken by others.

There is power in this to enrich our silent prayer. It cultivates the outward-focused attentiveness we want. But beyond that is the hint of something infinitely greater. Ordinarily we are aware of our own words when we speak. Yet now you are in very truth speaking, yet not listening to yourself. And when you listen beyond yourself in this way your speaking becomes listening.

Now let me make a further suggestion. It is perhaps a mystical idea and I am not a mystical person. I have the spiritual sensitivity of an oak log, and I am sceptical about religious experience, which can be a self-induced fraud. But I do think this is possible. I have myself been on the edge of it, and I hope you may go further in. The thing is this. In the psalms you say your words but, stretching yourself beyond them, you hear the words of others praying with you. Now in the same way can you pray your own prayer in your mind but listen beyond yourself so that instead of your mind you know the mind of God?

God is all that is good. If you pray something truly good you can be sure it is in God's mind too. Pray well and you pray in unison with God.

Try that now. Listen. Listen beyond. Listen beyond your own voice. Listen beyond your own thoughts. Don't fake it. Don't put words into God's mouth. But listen beyond your own words, thoughts, feelings and prayers. God is there. And at length, in your dialogue with God in your innermost thoughts, you may come to hear God's thoughts and not your own. And won't that be wonderful?

8 minutes

1 Kings 19.11–13a

He said, 'Go out and stand on the mountain before the Lord, for the Lord is about to pass by.' Now there was a great wind, so strong that it was splitting mountains and breaking rocks in pieces before the Lord, but the Lord was not in the wind; and after the wind an earthquake, but the Lord was not in the earthquake; and after the earthquake a fire, but the Lord was not in the fire; and after the fire a sound of sheer silence. When Elijah heard it, he wrapped his face in his mantle and went out and stood at the entrance of the cave.

Question for reflection

Bearing in mind Augustine's teaching that if we have understood something then that is not God, what might it actually be like to hear God's voice?

Prayer

O God,
my ways are not your ways;
neither are my thoughts your thoughts:
so I ask for the grace
to listen beyond myself
and hear your voice.

Day 28

Portable Peace

Remember the introductory offer on Day 1? This is where you claim it.

This listening silence you have been practising with serious intent and regular commitment, at the same time in the same place every day, is portable. We are going to take the peace we find in our 10 minutes of intentional silent prayer out on to the street. When we are anxious or bored. When we have nothing else to do or too much to do. Travelling. At work. Out with friends. The silent world of present calm is always within reach.

It's not magic for it takes attention and practice and it doesn't always work. But it's also not magic in the sense that it does actually happen. We get better at slipping into that silent world whatever situation we are in. And we grow in confidence and hope. The sands shift less. We stand more firmly on the rock.

The first thing is to remember to do it.

Just that.

Remember to be still and know that God is God.

But it's hard. Harder for us than for our forebears. Today we always have something to absorb our attention and drive stillness out of our hearts. We will speak on Day 32 of how wonderful boredom is. But boredom is rare. If you don't have a smartphone, well done. But probably you do. If you have, please get into 'developer options' and set it to black and white. It will distract you less. But still. Even with nobody to talk to, no ads to read, no TV in the corner, no announcements, we have a world of distraction in our pocket.

Remembering to step into the world of silent peace is simple. But like many good simple things, it's also quite hard. So we have to take action.

The first thing is to value stillness. We live in a world that values action, sound, things, production, consumption. Pausing for silence can seem like a nothing. We need to reshape our table of values to see it as one of the most worthwhile ways to bestow our time and attention. Top tip: embed this reality in your mind by telling other people about it.

Then you have to remember it in the hurly burly of the day to day. You could write on the back of your hand 'LISTEN' or 'KEEP SILENCE' or 'BE AT PEACE'. Or a post-it note on your computer screen. Or a phone cover with 'Be still and know that God is God' embossed on it. If you plan your day, then make a note to be silent from time to time. Make it a task.

Ideally, though, it becomes habitual. A great way to embed this habit is to send yourself an email on 'delay'. Write to yourself saying 'When there is nothing to do, do nothing'. Then use 'mail options' to delay delivery by a couple of days. When it arrives read it, think about it and pray a little. Then send back to yourself on two-day delay again. When it's come round 20 or 30 times, it will go in.

However you do it, if you can get to the point where you remember in the course of the day when a pocket of blank space opens up not to waste it scrolling content but let it expand into the infinite space of silent prayer, then you're halfway there. We'll talk in the next few days about ways to shape these moments for good. The key is to be in them.

8 minutes

From John Greenleaf Whittier, 'Dear Lord and Father'

Drop thy still dews of quietness,
till all our strivings cease;
take from our souls the strain and stress,
and let our ordered lives confess
the beauty of thy peace.
Breathe through the heats of our desire
thy coolness and thy balm;
let sense be dumb, let flesh retire;
speak through the earthquake, wind, and fire,
O still small voice of calm.

Question for reflection

What practical steps could you take to ensure that when a few spare minutes open up in your day, you remember to reflect and pray?

Prayer

Lord of all life,
thank you
for the energy and variety
of the world you give me to live in:
amid the noise and movement
help me remember
to seek moments of silent rest
with you.

Day 29

Just Doing Nothing

Every few years there's a new trend from northern Europe that offers to take us back to a simpler, more wholesome way of life. Hygge. Lagom. Mysa. Swedish death cleaning. They come and go. But Niksen has legs in my view. Niksen is the Dutch art of doing nothing. So in principle it's very simple. Just do nothing. The starting point is do nothing active – don't read, listen to a podcast, write a list, tidy something. Then don't do any hard thinking. Don't try to remember things, figure things out, and so on. Just let the mind wander where it likes. Then, maybe, when it's easy, let go of even the mind wandering, think of nothing; but only if it's not a big deal.

That's the key, really. It's not a big deal.

On the face of it, Niksen offers the same challenges as silent prayer. Ideas occur. A bird in flight catches the eye. Memories surface. But that's OK! This isn't silent prayer. It's Niksen.

Olga Mecking, whose 2019 book launched the craze, says Niksen is about 'letting go of the outcome'. It is precisely not something to get good at, to master, to complete. It's doing nothing. In Niksen, we no longer have to concern ourselves with Dostoevsky's polar bear. If you think of a polar bear, think of a polar bear. It's fine. You're in Holland. Relax.

With Niksen, the stakes are a little lower. It's not officially prayer. This does not mean God is absent. God is always here, now. Indeed, prayer is going on all the time, as we shall see on Day 39. God may speak through our Niksen. But the urge we may have when praying to be on our best behaviour, to miss nothing, to push in, reach up, deepen, broaden, which, though right, can cramp our style: none of this is present when you just pop out for a bit of Niksen.

All of this makes Niksen supremely portable. You can slip it into your day whenever, for however long, without stretching or warming up.

After grappling for the last three or four weeks with the strange tail-chasing dynamic of silent prayer, the need to let go of letting go, intentionally being unintentional, not thinking about not thinking ... Niksen may come as a relief. During the day, when you remember to pause for some Niksen, if your mind wanders from time to time that's OK. It's your mind, your time.

Simply, when a pocket of unclaimed time opens up, don't check the news or WhatsApp, write a shopping list or do Wordle – do some nothing. It's easy. All that is needful is remembering to do it.

We do not lose touch with the deeper discipline, of course. We keep the regular, committed, high-stakes, daunting but life-giving daily time of silence (and, by the way, do keep at it – the day you think 'maybe I'll give it a miss' is a chance to push through and strengthen your power of listening; moments of resistance are moments of growth). But even the most dedicated athlete also goes for a walk in the woods.

Not only that, but Niksen and the deeper discipline feed each other. The more profound your regular practice of silent prayer, the more readily you enter a cheerful moment of Niksen on the Tube or between meetings or in the airline security queue. And the more Niksen you find time for, the more listening silence will become your normal state.

Then each morning when you sit and breathe, listening, here now, you start a little further up the mountain.

9 minutes

John Keats, letter to John Hamilton Reynolds, 19 February 1818

I have an idea that a Man might pass a very pleasant life in this manner – let him on any certain day read a certain Page of full Poesy or distilled Prose and let him wander with, and muse upon it, and reflect from it, and bring home to it, and prophesy upon it, and dream upon it … How happy is such a 'voyage of conception' … What delicious diligent Indolence! A doze upon a Sofa does not hinder it, and a nap upon Clover engenders ethereal finger-pointings – the prattle of a child gives it wings, and the converse of a middle age a strength to beat them …

Question for reflection

What would it mean for you to 'let go of the outcome' for 5 minutes?

Prayer

O God
everything came into being from you
and all good works and desires come from you:
thank you that I am not so important
that I need to be doing something all the time.

Day 30

Smiling

Let me tell you my favourite psychological experiment.

Ninety-two students from Illinois University participated in what they were told was a study about performing tasks with parts of the body they would not normally use. They had to rate the funniness of cartoons by writing a score with a pen. Sometimes they had to hold the pen with their lips, not pressing with their teeth. Sometimes they had to hold it with their teeth, not touching it with their lips.

The experimenters tallied up how funny the students thought the cartoons were, depending on how they were holding the pen when they rated them:

Funniness when rated holding pen in lips: 4.9
Funniness when rated holding pen in teeth: 5.5

The only difference is how they were holding the pen.

You try it: hold a pen with your lips (no pressure from your teeth) and with your teeth (no contact with lips). Notice the shape of your mouth. You are making the shape of a frown and then of a smile.

If you simply make your face into the shape of a smile, you find things funnier.

We are one thing, from scalp to toenails. If we are anxious, we become clumsy. If we are confident, we run faster. If we are in a good mood, we smile. But it works the other way too. How we move and conduct ourselves changes how we feel and think. The link between your mood and your manner is less like a string and more like a stick. It's not just that your mood pulls your face into a smile. To a degree, your smile pushes your mood into a sunnier place.

I'm not making this up. It's science.

A smile nudges us into cheerfulness and calm. It makes it easier to be at peace, easier to be receptive. It loosens the hold of our worries.

Try it with your Niksen.

As ever, any spare 3 minutes when you might get your phone out or read the *Metro*: do nothing. But this time, smile. Not a big performance. No need to try and smile with the eyes or the whole body. And don't overdo it. You don't want to freak out your fellow-passengers. Just keep your lips together and squeeze the corners of the mouth up and out. This will make your eyes crinkle up too. Don't push it. Just a small, comfortable, quietly beaming smile. Smile and do nothing. See what it's like.

Again, if we keep up the regular discipline of serious listening silence – every day come rain or shine – this is an end in itself. And again, we bring things back into our daily discipline from our more casual silence and listening in the day. We spoke on Day 24 about the gentle smile with which we invite our toddler thoughts to rush about less and be at ease. It's the same smile. Have that smile ready to help dissipate the ripples.

Also, you could just start with the smile. There must be a reason why the Dalai Lama is always smiling. My guess is it's not only because peace makes you smile, but also because smiling makes you peaceful. Try it now. The gentle beatific smile that lifts the mood on a bus journey and takes the edge off disappointment and anxiety.

Sit, breathe, listen, here, now, smiling. Daily silence is a discipline. Nobody says it has to be glum.

9 minutes

From Matthew Green, 'The Spleen'

To cure the mind's wrong bias, Spleen,
Some recommended the bowling-green;
Some, hilly walks; all, exercise;
Fling but a stone, the giant dies;
Laugh and be well. Monkeys have been
Extreme good doctors for the Spleen;
And kitten, if the humor hit,
Has harlequinned away the fit.

Question for reflection

When you have tried intentionally smiling more frequently – particularly in moments of repose, and also in moments of anxiety – what impact does it have on you and on others?

Prayer

O Lord my God
your joy is my strength:
teach me to rejoice
in the small things
in gentle things
in hidden things
in all things.

Day 31

Looking Out

Here's another way to enrich your Niksen. Another strand to weave into the habit of pausing to be still from time to time. Another part of what we need instead of content-scrolling on our smartphones and other dopamine-stimulating pastimes.

Pick a point in front of you. Choose a visual anchor: the edge of a window, a stain on the wall, a coat hook. Something solid but uninteresting. Not a picture, a clock or a poster. Gaze at it. Of course, you are also sitting and breathing well, alert but not anxious, and smiling gently – all this is becoming second nature.

Now as you continue to gaze at your mark, become aware of what is going on to the left and right. Don't move your head or your eyes. But attend.

How far out can you perceive without moving your eyeballs? Maybe you can't be sure what is there, but you see a colour, a movement, a shape. You may fill in the gaps with guess and memory. If there are several objects to left or right, can you perceive how many there are even if you can't be sure what they are?

Try it on a train. Fix your eyes on some solid dull fixture in the carriage. Your peripheral vision will effloresce with trees whizzing by outside, sudden vistas, station signage, and so on. More and more of your perception will go out to the sides.

What's this all about?

A good body of research shows that in stressful situations we can lose our peripheral vision. That makes sense. Danger threatens – you look at the threat and blot out everything else. Can it work the other way round? If you widen your vision and attend to the periphery, can that have a calming effect? You will find websites that tell you this though they don't refer to peer-reviewed journals, and some of them are a bit whacky. But we do know that the same two-way street between mental and physical works in the case of smiling. So why not here?

At any rate, it has no bad side effects. And there is a pleasing symmetry about smiling and using peripheral vision. You send your attention out to the sides, leaving calm at the centre. Try it and see if it works for you.

Using your peripheral vision makes your looking more like listening. You lose the dominating precision of sight. Instead, you have to be receptive and attentive to something you can't control. Using peripheral vision turns looking into gazing.

So here's how we take our habit of silence out on to the street. When a pocket of time opens up, leave the phone alone. Sit. Breathe. Send everything out to the sides – mouth in a gentle smile, perception stretching out into the periphery. Do nothing. It's your time. The stakes are low. Let go of the outcome. Breathe. Smile. Gaze. Be here now. And though you need not explicitly pray, when you are here, now, you can be sure that whatever and whoever else is here, now, God is always here, now.

If you're taking my advice then you won't be able to use your peripheral vision in your 9 minutes of intentional silence this morning. Or won't you? Try looking at the farthest corners of the insides of your eyelids. Try it with the gentle smile. Spread your energy out, leaving calm at the centre.

9 minutes

Psalm 121

I lift up my eyes to the hills;
from where is my help to come?
My help comes from the Lord,
the maker of heaven and earth.

Question for reflection

When you have tried a few times attending to peripheral vision when anxious or in some other negative state, do you notice any effect on your frame of mind?

Prayer

Holy Spirit,
source of all life and desire,
help me to see
the full breadth
of this strange and wonderful world,
that I may know how little I am,
how little depends on me.

Day 32

Embrace Boredom

Were you bored yesterday? If you like, that can be the last day you were ever bored.

You know how this works by now. An occasion for boredom is an opportunity.

What bores you? Nothing to do? A repetitive task? Someone explaining something you already know? A long bus ride? What are the situations where you think 'I'm bored'? Those are the situations you need. Bring it on. Now is your chance to lean in, to take full advantage of the opportunity to be here, now, listening in prayerful silence – then you are no longer bored.

Nothing to do. Fabulous! Sit. Stand if you can't sit, but stand well. Breathe (if you can't breathe, that's a bigger problem which I suggest you deal with at once) and breathe well, with attention. Listen. Close your eyes if it won't look weird. Otherwise, attend to peripheral vision. You are here, now. Whatever and whoever else is here, now, God is always here, now.

A repetitive task? Excellent! Attend. Hear the sounds you make as you work. Feel the textures of the things you handle. Let the visual detail come to you. Breathe well, aware of your lungs filling and emptying, aware of your whole body. God is here, now.

That person you often try to avoid is going on and on. What luck! Well, be realistic, at some point you will also want techniques to get out of this situation with grace and compassion. For that you need another book. I'm here to tell you this is also a great opportunity to strengthen your powers of listening. And also to give a gift. Perhaps this person doesn't deserve a gift, but does any of us? All have sinned and fall short of the glory of God, and all are justified through his free gift. So give the gift. Attend. Not thinking what to say next. Not thinking how to get out of it. Just listening to each word. Even if you don't in the end find the conversation edifying, I guarantee it's more joyful if you listen.

A long bus ride. Niksen city! Wriggle about to get your posture right. Breathe well. Let go of the outcome. Gaze. Smile. Peripheral vision. What's not to like? You'll wish there were more stops.

Come on, I told you this was going to be fun.

And this is not to deny or disparage the great profundity at its core. As we embrace the opportunities offered by those situations that used to menace us with boredom, we deepen our capacity for listening silence. But God is the God of yes, not of no. God became one of us in the form of a man who liked a good walk and a picnic with his friends and could crack a joke. This sober, disciplined practice of regular silent prayer feeds a day-to-day life that is light-hearted and open.

9 minutes

Philippians 4.12–13

I know what it is to have little, and I know what it is to have plenty. In any and all circumstances I have learned the secret of being well-fed and of going hungry, of having plenty and of being in need. I can do all things through him who strengthens me.

Question for reflection

What is it, really, that you don't like about 'being bored'?

Prayer

Lord Jesus,
you fasted forty days in the wilderness
and afterwards angels ministered to you:
give me strength to go on through the desert
and find your peace.

Day 33

Walking Away from the Looking Glass House

So far, so self-centred. This has been about silent prayer that you, singular, practise daily. I have spoken of my own experience of listening silence. We have seen how each of us can weave the discipline through the rest of the day so as to live better.

Good. It's OK to pursue these things. But remember the dynamic we have met again and again? We strive intentionally and actively not to act, intend or strive. We hold fast to letting go. It is the human condition. That distinctive human condition that arises from being amphibians living in both the material and the spiritual. We all reckon with this, which is why again and again we read in the Scriptures:

- God chose what is foolish in the world to shame the wise (1 Cor. 1.27).
- I regard everything as loss because of the surpassing value of knowing Christ Jesus my Lord (Phil. 3.8).
- All who exalt themselves will be humbled, and those who humble themselves will be exalted (Luke 14.11).
- He has filled the hungry with good things, and sent the rich away empty (Luke 1.53).
- Those who want to save their life will lose it, and those who lose their life for my sake, and for the sake of the gospel, will save it (Mark 8.35).
- If we have died with him, we will also live with him (2 Tim. 2.11).

- The last will be first, and the first will be last (Matt. 20.16).

It's a fundamental gospel truth that comes into all of our lives, but which comes to a very sharp point in silent prayer. As a wise man once said to me, the cross of Christ is 'I' crossed out.
  If this be so, then we need to turn ourselves outwards. That way lies true peace and joy. But if we turn ourselves outwards in order to get the peace and the joy for ourselves, we will find we are just turning in on ourselves. We really have to turn our back on self in order to find ourselves. And as we have seen in these last weeks, turning our back on ourselves is not that easy.
  If the disciplined practice of silent listening prayer is good for anything, it is good as a way to self-forgetfulness. Not oblivion, but the very opposite. We do not blot out ourselves or the world around us. We enter fully into both by turning our attention outwards. In listening silence we practise and learn the great Christian virtue of humility, the soil, the humus, in which all the other virtues grow. In listening we enter into that self-emptying *kenosis* of which St Paul writes in Philippians 2: seek the same mind that was in Christ Jesus, who, though he was in the form of God ... emptied himself, taking the form of a slave ... humbled himself and became obedient to the point of death.
  Kenosis. Self-emptying. Humility. Obedience. Listening trains us in these powerful, life-giving, Christ-like virtues.
  In this last week we turn our listening intentionally outwards. And today in our time of silence, we reach cruising altitude. From now on it's always the same: 10 minutes a day, day by day, decade by decade.

10 minutes

Romans 7.21–25

So I find it to be a law that when I want to do what is good, evil lies close at hand. For I delight in the law of God in my inmost self, but I see in my members another law at war with the law of my mind, making me captive to the law of sin that dwells in my members. Wretched man that I am! Who will rescue me from this body of death? Thanks be to God through Jesus Christ our Lord!

Question for reflection

What are the things in your life that really give you joy, and how did they become part of your life?

Prayer

Jesus my Saviour
you let go of your own life
and rose imperishable:
help me to loosen my grasp
on what I want
and open my hands to receive from you
what I need.

Day 34

Because the Other is Worth It

L'Oreal have used the same slogan to sell cosmetics since 1971: 'Because I'm worth it'. This and the consumer culture it typifies is something we stand against when we listen.

'Because I'm worth it.'

It's interesting that this is the slogan of a cosmetics company. Cosmetics are very visual and, as we have seen, our sense of sight lends itself to getting what we want, pursuing our own purposes, manipulating our environment.

When we listen we say instead:

'Because the other person is infinitely worthwhile.'

In listening we are attentive, open, willing to be changed, to take a risk, to be for others. If you wanted to console, encourage or uplift someone, would you look, or would you listen? Has anybody ever said, of someone who gave comfort in time of trouble, 'she's such a great looker'? One of the best things about being resolute in your practice of silent listening prayer is that it helps you be that most wonderful thing, a good listener.

All of us at some time find ourselves face to face with someone in distress. Clergy more often than most, perhaps. But all of us from time to time. So you are with a fellow human being in the grip of sorrow, fear, loss or hopelessness. There may be delusion. There may be rage. There may be terrible unsayable sadness. Or it may be all too obvious what is the matter. A husband, wife or child has died an untimely death. A terminal illness has taken hold. There has been a terrible betrayal.

Here you are with this other person for whom you want the best. And what is the first thought? The thought that makes the hair stand up on the back of your neck like the creak of a door in an empty house at night?

'What on earth can I say?'

The flywheels and pistons of the mind whirr faster and faster, seeking something to grind into healing words that will soothe the pain, make sense of the sorrow, fill the empty void of loss. And really if nothing comes to mind and we are left dumb, that may be for the best. The graveside or the waiting room in the Intensive Care Unit is not the place for good advice. Yet still the flywheel spins, the panic rises. What, in the face of this unknowable, immense sorrow can I offer that will do justice to the situation?

You can guess where I am going with this.

What is the one thing we need to remember when the temptation to fill the void with words becomes unbearable, when the insistent question comes again and again in the mind, 'What on earth can I say?'

Listen.

Just that.

Listen.

Except, not *just that*. For listening is never 'just listening'. It is hard work calling for intense concentration. And it is risky. To listen deeply, not guessing what will be said or thinking what to say next, not assessing or analysing, is to put ourselves in the power of the person we listen to. We are there for them, not for ourselves. We are not in control of the situation. This is at the heart of what we have to give. Like listening in the psalms, we listen so we don't hear ourselves at all. If we are brave enough we empty ourselves, taking the very nature of a servant.

This is a great gift to give in time of trouble, but the capacity for this kind of listening is something we have to cultivate with committed, regular practice.

You know what to do.

10 minutes

Philippians 2.5–8

Let the same mind be in you that was in Christ Jesus,
who, though he was in the form of God,
did not regard equality with God
as something to be exploited,
but emptied himself,
taking the form of a slave,
being born in human likeness.
And being found in human form,
he humbled himself
and became obedient to the point of death –
even death on a cross.

Question for reflection

When has someone else really listened to you?

Prayer

Lord Jesus,
you heal the sick and encourage the fearful:
in listening to my brothers and sisters
with keen and patient love,
may I be a channel of your peace.

Day 35

Listening Outward

We don't give up on speech in challenging conversations. But if there is a truly comforting or wise word to say, it only comes to our lips out of the kind of silence we have been practising. It is not going to be an answer to the anxious question 'What on *earth* can I say?' The good thing to say that comes from true, prayerful, listening silence will not be bound to Earth.

Most often, though, it is simply in the listening that we offer what God has to give through us. In listening we open up space and time for sorrow to breathe, for pain to stretch itself and find relief, for fear to find the comforting light. If we listen deep and true, the person we listen to may hear words they need from their own lips. If we listen we are present and the other person will know this. It will not fix everything. But it will be a gift. It is the way to say truly without words 'you are not alone'.

But it is not only at moments of crisis that we can give this gift. Are we at a badly prepared presentation from an anxious colleague? We listen. At least it will be an exercise in mindfulness, strengthening the muscles of attention. But also through listening will come interest, ideas, community. And the anxious colleague will not feel abandoned or despised: he or she may even get confidence from our listening to say something interesting.

Are we in conflict? Is someone ranting and accusing? Listen. A deeply Christian response. Not weak, passive or dishonourable. But also not aggressive or dignified. Listening is how we love our enemies. And as we listen in self-emptying silence, we may find that the bad things the other person says cease to be darts shot into our heart. They are simply words to which we attend. Maybe we even find there is some truth, something to learn, some need to change or be contrite. Even if we don't learn something about ourself, we will learn something about the person speaking if we will listen.

Then again with our friends, what a lovely gift to listen as they pour out their hearts, chat about their hopes and their holidays. How loved they are, how loved they will know themselves to be. It must be listening: not waiting our turn to say our thing but concentrating without agenda on the person. Or with children. What can one say to a child? Often not much. They do not always attend or understand. But one can always listen. Listen with wonder and delight, with deep attention, with joy and courtesy, drawing out of them their own self-understanding, helping them to find out who they are in their own words.

In the streets: we listen.

On the phone to the call centre: we listen.

As the plumber explains what needs to be done – though we may not understand a single word: we listen.

Receiving directions or instructions: we listen.

When we have nothing to say round the table: we listen.

In our daily 10 minutes of committed, intentional silence we are learning this skill, strengthening this muscle, developing the capacity to be present, attending with humility and love, emptying ourselves to be filled with a God-given understanding of the other: not calculating, not planning, not grasping; listening, here, now.

10 minutes

From Thomas Carlyle, *Memoirs of the Life of Scott*

Under all speech that is good for any thing there lies a silence that is better. Silence is deep as eternity; speech is shallow as time. Paradoxical does it seem? Woe for the age, woe for the man, quack-ridden, bespeeched, bespouted, blown about like barren Sahara, to whom this world-old truth were altogether strange!

Question for reflection

Think about the many different situations in which you will find yourself in the coming days, how many of them could become better and deeper and more joyful through listening?

Prayer

Holy Spirit
giver of good gifts,
thank you for the gift of listening:
may I live outward,
with love and keen attention,
and give that gift again
to those among whom you place me.

Day 36

Pre-flight Checklist

We are in our last week together. Thank you for coming this far. Soon you will go on without me.

In our final four days together we shall dig into what this is really about – the One to whom we listen. Then it's over to you. My prayer for you is that you will be steadfast; that you will persevere. It is just 10 minutes a day. SBLHN. Sit, Breathe, Listen, Here, Now. Same time, same place, day after day, decade after decade. Something good is going to happen.

No need to complexify it. Mark Rippetoe, the barbell prophet, says a good thing which reads straight across from the gym to the practice of silent prayer. He says we face a two-fold challenge: 'It's hard to train this way, and people don't like difficult things – yet it's simple, and people don't think simple things can work.'

As so often with what is truly life-giving, silent prayer is not that complicated. It's just quite hard.

That said, there are things to learn. Simple habits that become instinctual so that when you start you are ready, when your mind wanders you are naturally cued to coax it back. And although these things are simple, we do have to work to internalize them. We can't pause our silence to look things up in a book, for reading a book is not silent prayer. We need these simple practices in our very bones.

So here's a parting gift. A checklist. Read it from time to time when you have 5 minutes to let it sink in. Maybe rewrite it to add things you find helpful and shape it to work for you. But try this for now. At this point, it will not be new to you – but it needs to become second nature:

- ☐ Sit: alert not tense, balanced, grounded, no pressure points, forearms on thighs, hands loosely together.
- ☐ Breathe: fill the lungs from the bottom, the belly a dome, chest out, ribs out; breathe out from the bottom of the lungs.
- ☐ Be here, now. Make this your intention. Keep coming back to it.
- ☐ Have words of Scripture so familiar that you don't need to say them. Let them come to mind when needed. Mine are 'speak, for your servant is listening'; 'be still and know that I am God'. Write yours down when you know what they are.
- ☐ Be ready when the mind wanders:
  - smile gently and invite yourself back to the centre
  - attend to the breath and be sure you are breathing well
  - be aware of the body: maybe a body scan?
- ☐ Be alert for moments of balance when you can truly be here, now; for example:
  - between breathing in and breathing out
  - between breathing out and breathing in
  - at the midpoint in the psalm
- ☐ Listen beyond yourself, attending not to your thoughts but to the ideal of your thoughts in the mind of God.
- ☐ When out and about in the hurly-burly of the everyday:
  - when there is nothing to do, do nothing
  - let go of the outcome
  - smile
  - attend to peripheral vision
  - embrace boredom as an opportunity
- ☐ Bring what you experience when out and about back into your times of intentional silence.
- ☐ Above all, before all, under all:
  - listen
  - listen
  - listen

Now, 10 more minutes please. The same as yesterday. The same as tomorrow. SBLHN – Sit, Breathe, Listen, Here, Now …

10 minutes

From Rudyard Kipling, 'The 'Eathen'

An' now the hugly bullets come peckin' through the dust,
An' no one wants to face 'em, but every beggar must;
So, like a man in irons, which isn't glad to go,
They moves 'em off by companies uncommon stiff an' slow.

Of all 'is five years' schoolin' they don't remember much
Excep' the not retreatin', the step an' keepin' touch.
It looks like teachin' wasted when they duck an' spread an'
 'op -
But if 'e 'adn't learned 'em they'd be all about the shop.

Question for reflection

Are you going to keep going with this?

Prayer

God of all time and eternity,
help me to keep walking towards you
following the Way that is Christ
hand in hand with you
day by day.

Day 37

Listening Towards

It's a risky business, though, listening. It can call for courage. In that situation we talked about where you listen to someone in distress, it takes courage to face down the self-accusation 'you're not doing anything, you're just listening'. And always, when we listen we give ourselves. We make ourselves available. In listening to someone else we make that person matter as much as we do, but that puts us in their power to a degree. This is good, right and powerful, precisely the Christlike thing to do. Yet we remember that the way of Christ is the way of the cross.

There is something important at the heart of this. There is a virtue we have lost sight of in the twenty-first century. A virtue we think of as a weakness, perhaps even a vice, but which we need more of. It is intertwined with listening silent prayer. I don't know if you will like it. You may feel I have sneaked this one up on you. You thought this was about listening and you were right. But listening is more than you think.

It is, as we have seen, an alert, attentive hearing. Not just sitting with our ears open. It is directed, intentional hearing. Hearing towards. In Latin 'to hear' is *audire* and 'towards' is *ob*. To 'hear towards' is *ob-audire*. This is where our word 'obey' comes from. To obey is to hear towards, to hear attentively – in short, to listen. And our word 'listen' comes from the Old Norse word *hlust*; and, ultimately, it goes back thousands of years and is related to the Sanskrit *srusti*, which means 'obedience'.

Listening is obedience.

This goes to the heart of why listening is so countercultural, so subversive, and also so unfashionable. When we really listen we practise the virtue of obedience. We do not seek to control what is said. Real silent listening does not use what is said as ammunition. We do not assess or plan or think what to say next. We open ourselves to what comes from someone else, willing to be changed or moved.

When parents say their children 'don't listen' they really mean their children 'don't obey'. For to listen in truth is to become obedient. Obedience of children to parents as well as mutual obedience between friends and colleagues, and between husband and wife, is wholesome and well worth practising. But the most life-giving and essential obedience is to God.

We have to go beyond hearing God in the Scriptures or elsewhere, but then going our own way. Hearing we can do without understanding, or being changed. We can hear without obeying. It is risk-free but empty. Instead, we need listening silence that is so open to God that God's will becomes our will. The more we listen to God, the more obedient we become. Indeed, if we are not obedient, we probably haven't listened.

As Jesus says in Luke 11.28, 'Blessed ... are those who hear the word of God and obey it!' And remember what Mary says when the Angel tells her she is to be the mother of God – 'Here am I, the servant of the Lord; let it be with me according to your word' (Luke 1.38).

10 minutes

Gerard Manley Hopkins, 'Heaven-Haven: A Nun Takes the Veil'

I have desired to go
Where springs not fail,
To fields where flies no sharp and sided hail
And a few lilies blow.
And I have asked to be
Where no storms come,
Where the green swell is in the havens dumb,
And out of the swing of the sea.

Question for reflection

Are you willing to be obedient to God?

Prayer

God our father,
maker of all,
ruler of all:
give me ears to hear you
and a heart to obey.

Day 38

The Listening God

The aim of this book has been to help you acquire and deepen the habit of silent listening prayer. So far, we have spoken of this silent listening as something going on within. But that is not all that is going on. It is not even the most interesting thing that is going on. Coming to the end of the first leg of this infinite journey is the time to be explicit about where the journey leads, and about the foundations of the road we tread. The most surprising and important thing about your silent listening prayer is not that you are silent, listening.

The really big thing is: God listens.

We are right if we find this strange. God is King. All wisdom and might are in his hands. What reason has he for listening to us? It is the part of kings to command, not to listen. Yet we know God does listen.

Some psalms even begin 'Incline your ear, O Lord' (Ps. 86) – a strange and dangerous thing to say to a king you might think. We have a picture of God lowering, but also opening, his ear. Coming down to our level? Or humbling himself?

It is when he hears the groaning of the people that God acts to free them from slavery in Egypt. And in the promised land they sing their psalms, confident that God listens: 'the Lord has heard my weeping, The Lord has heard my cry for mercy' (Ps. 6.9); 'From his temple he heard my voice; my cry came before him' (Ps. 18.6); 'you heard my cry for mercy when I called to you' (Ps. 31.22); 'I waited patiently for the Lord; he turned to me and heard my cry' (Ps. 40.1).

And as God is God who listens, when he ceases to listen then something serious has occurred. The people make their worship a formality empty of love for God and neighbour, and God says, 'I take no delight in your solemn assemblies ... I will not listen to the melody of your harps' (Amos 5.21, 23). The Psalmist begs 'you are my Rock, do not turn a deaf ear to me' (Ps. 28.1), then rejoices in relief: 'Praise be to the Lord, for he has heard my cry for mercy' (Ps. 28.6). When God turns his ear from us it is a sign things have gone badly wrong, for it is his nature to listen.

God's listening is a sign of that risk-taking, self-giving love we know in its highest form in the journey into the strange country that God's Son made, emptying himself on the cross so that we could live his new life when he rose from the tomb. And again we are right if this surprises us. It was not what anybody expected from God. A listening God is foolishness to Gentiles, if not a stumbling block to Jews. But God's listening is a gift. God's listening is God's grace.

Now, as you sit, breathe, and listen, here, now, know for certain that God listens to you. No need to ponder too deeply for you will not get to the bottom of it. Simply wonder at it. Know that it is remarkable and surprising: a gift.

10 minutes

Psalm 29

The voice of the Lord flashes forth flames of fire.
The voice of the Lord shakes the wilderness;
the Lord shakes the wilderness of Kadesh.
The voice of the Lord causes the oaks to whirl,
and strips the forest bare;
and in his temple all say, 'Glory!'
The Lord sits enthroned over the flood;
the Lord sits enthroned as king for ever.
May the Lord give strength to his people!
May the Lord bless his people with peace!

Question for reflection

What do you want God to hear?

Prayer

Almighty God,
in Jesus Christ
you gave yourself to us
so that we could know you and love you:
so I am bold enough to pray,
hear me when I call to you.

Day 39

The Life of God

God listens. We listen. And again, this calls for reflection. On the face of it, this sounds like a dull conversation. God and me sitting in silence like that awkward moment at the school reunion when you wonder what you and this other person used to talk about. Surely if both listen, nothing is going on?

But it is not so. It is the very opposite. That space of prayer in which we listen and God listens is dense, charged, filled with abundant life.

First, of course, God does not always just listen. God speaks. We never forget this. We long for it and if we hear the voice of God we rejoice. If that is what your regular disciplined practice of silent prayer brings, your time was well spent. Though we also reflect, testing against the Scriptures, and in conversation with our friends, whose voice this really is.

But besides the speech of God, something else may happen in that silent space where God listens and you listen.

God listens. You listen. And this is prayer.

But if we think this is a blank and dull kind of prayer we are forgetting the very heart of Christian theology. God is Trinity. When you listen and God listens, there is One other who is not other, who may speak too.

God listens. We listen. And as we listen to the faint rustle of the wider world, the gentle movement of our breath, the occasional gurglings of our bodies, the silent movements of our thoughts, attending to what is here, now; as we listen and as God listens, though there is here just God and us, there is Another who may speak for us and through us and to us, through whom we may speak the true words of who we really are, through whom without words we may come to know.

You may already have in mind the wonderful verses from St Paul's letters to the Romans to which all of this refers:

> ... the Spirit helps us in our weakness; for we do not know how to pray as we ought, but that very Spirit intercedes with sighs too deep for words. And God, who searches the heart, knows what is the mind of the Spirit, because the Spirit intercedes for the saints according to the will of God. (Rom. 8.26–27)

This is the heart of true prayer. Prayer is always going on. Prayer was going on before the universe was made. For prayer is simply the inner life of God, Father, Son and Holy Spirit in perfect unity. If our silent prayer is true prayer, it is so because through it we are caught up in this. If it's not too humdrum an image for this infinite mystery, prayer is like an escalator. It is always going whether we are on it or not. We may walk up the escalator with our spoken, felt prayers. But in silent prayer we simply step on to the escalator and let it carry us.

Please reflect on this before you begin your 10 minutes today, and then as you enter into silence be open to being drawn into the life of God.

10 minutes

Romans 8.19–28

For the creation waits with eager longing for the revealing of the children of God; for the creation was subjected to futility, not of its own will but by the will of the one who subjected it, in hope that the creation itself will be set free from its bondage to decay and will obtain the freedom of the glory of the children of God. We know that the whole creation has been groaning in labour pains until now; and not only the creation, but we ourselves, who have the first fruits of the Spirit, groan inwardly while we wait for adoption, the redemption of our bodies. For in hope we were saved. Now hope that is seen is not hope. For who hopes for what is seen? But if we hope for what we do not see, we wait for it with patience. Likewise the Spirit helps us in our weakness; for we do not know how to pray as we ought, but that very Spirit intercedes with sighs too deep for words. And God, who searches the heart, knows what is the mind of the Spirit, because the Spirit intercedes for the saints according to the will of God. We know that all things work together for good for those who love God, who are called according to his purpose.

Question for reflection

What would it be like to enter into the eternal life of prayer that is God, Father, Son and Holy Spirit?

Prayer
(adapted from the *Common Worship Daily Prayer* post-communion prayer for Trinity Sunday)

Holy God,
faithful and unchanging:
enlarge my mind with the knowledge of your truth,
and draw me more deeply into the mystery of your love,
that I may truly worship you,
Father, Son and Holy Spirit.

Day 40

No Longer I that Liveth

Thank you for coming this far. If you will keep to this, 10 minutes a day, sitting, breathing, listening, here, now – it will be so good for you. It may seem too little a thing to matter so much. But we have seen that even this little is not easy.

At least, I do not find it so. Perhaps you have long since learnt to step at will into a state of pure attention, fully present, at peace, beyond time, free of anxiety, striving or regret. May it be so! If not, though, I hope you agree that a true 10 minutes a day of silent prayer is substantial enough to be worth doing. Please persevere. As ever, it is not that complicated, just hard. And what makes it hard is what makes it worth continuing with.

All through these 40 days we have come back again and again to the paradox at the heart of silent prayer. Silent prayer is not the silence of oblivion. We aspire to be more present than at other times. Yet all the ways of being present we are used to involve doing, speaking, thinking and so on. Now we lay down that whole toolkit. But it contains the only tools we have to accomplish anything, including the act of laying down. So we strive not to strive, hold fast to letting go, intend to relinquish our intentions.

So far, so familiar. But now let me tell you this is not just a challenge in silent prayer. It is a challenge that silent prayer brings into focus and can help us to meet. But it is the challenge in the whole of the Christian life. God has given us our lives. The journey of this lifetime is to give our lives back to him so that we will truly live. God wants us to be both perfect but also ourselves. He can make us perfect at once by obliterating us, making us happy robots. But he has chosen the longer way, setting us free in hope that in time we learn to use our God-given freedom in the only good way, giving our wills to the will of God.

This is what St Paul means when he writes in Romans 8.19–21 of the creation subjected to futility (the perverse uses to which we put our freedom), waiting with eager longing for the revelation of the glorious freedom of the children of God. May your silent prayer bring you to this glorious freedom. May the daily discipline of 10 minutes sitting, breathing, listening, here, now, grow deeper, broader and truer as the years go by. And as you listen beyond yourself to God, as God listens with you, may the Spirit speak in and through you. Then may it be no longer you that lives, but Christ who lives in you, that you may truly live.

10 minutes

Galatians 2.20

... and it is no longer I who live, but it is Christ who lives in me. And the life I now live in the flesh I live by faith in the Son of God, who loved me and gave himself for me.

Question for reflection

Who do you long to become?

Prayer

Lord Jesus Christ
you became human
that we might become divine:
as I listen in your Spirit,
help me to grow into your likeness.

Further Reading

Readings from the psalms are taken from *Common Worship Daily Prayer*, but other biblical texts are from the NRSVA. All poems, hymns and other texts are widely anthologized or available online. There are some links to these and other texts, with material to help you use this book in different ways, at seasonofsilence.org.

This Further Reading section gives you references to some of the texts I quote in the book that I think would be worth your while digging into further, or which need a little commentary, and some suggestions for further reading on silent prayer.

Common Worship Daily Prayer (London: Church House Publishing, 2005). This book offers a structure of daily prayer that is simple enough for everyone to do it, yet rich in detail and seasonal variation. It is also a useful compendium of some of the most wonderful verses in Scripture, and some of the deepest prayers Christians have ever prayed; and it has a beautifully laid-out Psalter.

Matthew Arnold, 'Dover Beach'. Like the others, this poem is widely anthologized, and available online, but I want to say something more about it here. It's a good poem, but Arnold was stuck in a heedless pessimism. The stanza quoted evokes well the daunting emptiness with which silence may confront us. But when Arnold then goes on in the rest of the poem to reflect on the sea of faith which was once at the full, retreating down the naked shingles, he misses the deep meaning of his own metaphor. Yes, the tide has gone out and it's night so you can't see the sea. But the sea is still there. And what do we know about the tide? It comes back in.

St Benedict, *Rule*. The foundational text of Western monasticism, 1,500 years after it was composed, is still the foundation of most Christian religious communities. There are many translations and editions; I have quoted from that made available online by the Abbey of Solesmes: www.solesmes.com/sites/default/files/upload/pdf/rule_of_st_benedict.pdf (accessed 9.05.2025).

Anthony Bloom, *Beginning to Pray* (Mahwah, NJ: Paulist Press, 1970). ++Anthony, an Orthodox Archbishop, was Metropolitan of Great Britain and Ireland. As a young man he served in the French Resistance and was arrested by the Gestapo. The book is a straightforward, practical guide to contemplative prayer.

Robin Daniels, *Listening: Hearing the Heart* (Watford: Instant Apostle, 2016). Daniels is a psychotherapist and this book has much to teach us about the healing power of listening silence.

Fyodor Dostoevsky, tran. R. L. Renfield, *Winter Notes on Summer Impressions* (New York: Criterion Books, 1955). This is not primarily a text on contemplative prayer, but is full of insight on so many topics, and is a helpful perspective that is self-consciously critical of the way the Western world thought in the nineteenth century, which is probably yet more pertinent in the twenty-first.

T. S. Eliot, *Four Quartets*. Again, there are many editions: I used the Faber Library facsimile of the 1944 edition. See particularly 'Burnt Norton', II, p. 5, and 'East Coker', III, p. 16. But there is so much wisdom in this poem about silence, listening, searching and letting go (and so much else) that I wish you would read it all, again and again.

Evagrius Ponticus, tran. J. E. Bamberger, *The Praktikos* and *Chapters on Prayer* (Trappist, KY: Cistercian Publications, 1972). Evagrius was a fourth-century monk from what is now Northern Turkey, and a mystic and an ascetic. This is a short book of challenging advice, pithy but deep. Read a sentence a day.

Walter Hilton, tran. L. Sherley-Price, *The Ladder of Perfection* (London: Penguin, 1988). A classic of English spiritual writing, replete with wisdom on the search for God in contemplative prayer.

Irenaeus of Lyons, *Against Heresies*. Irenaeus, roughly contemporary with Marcus Aurelius, was a bishop and one of the earliest Trinitarian theologians – a very wise theologian who recognized that all theology must tail off into mystery in the end. Victorian translations of his writings are freely available online in the New Advent Catholic Encyclopaedia: the passage from which I quoted is here: https://www.newadvent.org/fathers/0103506.htm (accessed 9.05.2025).

Jamie Kreiner, *The Wandering Mind: What Medieval Monks Tell Us About Distraction* (London: W. W. Norton & Co., 2023). A well-resourced study, drawing on original sources to take us into the lives of monks and nuns from several centuries of the Church, and shows how they struggled, sometimes successfully, to transcend distraction; it offers helpful lessons, and a delightful insight into the familiar humanity of those who went before us.

Martin Laird, *Into the Silent Land* (London: Darton, Longman and Todd, 2006). A modern classic – it covers quite similar territory to the book now in your hands, but Martin Laird is a learned theologian and a profound thinker. Read this one next.

C. S. Lewis, *Screwtape Letters*. Full of practical wisdom on how to live God's way in a fallen world, couched as advice from an older demon to a younger one on how to corrupt a human. Many editions are available. The passage I quote (by permission) on Day 6 is from the 1946 Centenary Press edition.

Marcus Aurelius, *Meditations*. Marcus was a Roman emperor in the second century but we remember him now more for this wonderful and wise book. It is one of the key texts of Stoicism, a school of philosophy that taught the cultivation of virtue as the way to inner peace. It has much to offer you as you explore silent prayer. A good modern translation is by Gregory Hays (New York: Random House Modern Library Paperback, 2002). The passage I quoted (in my own translation) is on p. 37 of the Hays edition.

Diarmaid MacCulloch, *Silence, A Christian History* (London: Penguin, 2014). MacCulloch is one of the greatest living church historians: this short (by his standards!) and very readable book is a survey of the Christian understanding and practice of silence over 2,000 years.

Adam S. McHugh, *The Listening Life: Embracing Attentiveness in a World of Distraction* (Downers Grove, IL: InterVarsity Press, 2015). Accessible and optimistic – it is particularly helpful on how we can turn contemplation outwards as part of a whole life.

Olga Mecking, *Niksen: Embracing the Dutch Art of Doing Nothing* (London: Piatkus, 2020). The book that launched the Niksen craze.

Cal Newport, *Deep Work* (London: Piatkus, 2016). A very practical book, with a focus on the professional world, but much to offer in all areas of life, focusing on how we can resist and overcome the daunting array of amped-up distractions with which early twenty-first-century life surrounds us.

Leonid Ouspensky, *Theology of the Icon* (Crestwood, NY: St Vladimir's Seminary Press, 1978). A comprehensive introduction to the use of icons in contemplative prayer.

Mark Rippetoe, *Starting Strength* (Wichita Falls, TX: Aasgaard Company, 2011). Anyone who would like real core strength could not do better than follow his programme. He is also very pungent on the merits of persistence and simplicity, and this reads across very well from physical to spiritual disciplines. The line about aversion to good things that are simple and hard is actually from his blog: https://startingstrength.com/article/deep_squats (accessed 9.05.2025).

F. Strack, S. Stepper, S. and L. L. Martin, 'Inhibiting and Facilitating Conditions of the Human Smile: A Nonobtrusive Test of the Facial Feedback Hypothesis', *Journal of Personality and Social Psychology* (1988, vol. 54, no. 5, pp. 768–77). Scientific proof that smiling makes you cheerful!

Thich Nhat Hanh, trans. Mobi Ho, *The Miracle of Mindfulness* (Boston, MA: Beacon Press, 1987). A clear and accessible introduction to Buddhist practice, which a Christian can read with integrity (no creed, no conflict, as they say – though we heed the advice of 1 Cor. 8) – lots of good helpful stuff on attending to the breath.

But you know, '… the kingdom of God depends not on talk but on power' as St Paul says (1 Cor. 4.20). Salutary as good reading is, it is not silent prayer. It may be an aid but must never be a distraction from sitting, breathing and listening, here, now.

www.ingramcontent.com/pod-product-compliance
Lightning Source LLC
Chambersburg PA
CBHW060612080526
44585CB00013B/788